TWAYNE'S WORLD AUTHORS SERIES

A Survey of the World's Literature

Sylvia E. Bowman, Indiana University

GENERAL EDITOR

GERMANY

Ulrich Weisstein, Indiana University

EDITOR

Günter Grass

(TWAS 65)

TWAYNE'S WORLD AUTHORS SERIES (TWAS)

*The purpose of TWAS is to survey the major writers
—novelists, dramatists, historians, poets, philosophers,
and critics—of the nations of the world. Among the
national literatures covered are those of Australia,
Canada, China, Eastern Europe, France, Germany,
Greece, Italy, Japan, Latin America, New Zealand,
Poland, Russia, Scandinavia, Spain, and the African
nations, as well as Hebrew, Yiddish, and Latin Classical literature. This survey is complemented by
Twayne's United States Authors Series and
English Authors Series.*

*The intent of each volume in these series is to present
a critical-analytical study of the works of the writer;
to include biographical and historical material that
may be necessary for understanding, appreciation,
and critical appraisal of the writer; and to present all
material in clear, concise English—but not to vitiate
the scholarly content of the work by doing so.*

Günter Grass

By W. GORDON CUNLIFFE
University of Wisconsin

Twayne Publishers, Inc.   ::   New York

12-17-69

Contents

Chronology

1927   Grass born on October 16, in Danzig, where his parents kept a small retail grocery.

1933–   Attends elementary school (*Volksschule*) and high school
1944   (*Gymnasium*) in Danzig. Towards the end of this period, he serves as an anti-aircraft gunner and in the Labor Service.

1944–   Soldier. Wounded during Russian advance. At military hos-
1945   pital in Marienbad. Prisoner-of-war of the American forces in Bavaria for a few months.

1946   Released from imprisonment. Temporary employment as farm worker in the Rhineland and worker in a potash mine.

1947   Apprentice stone carver for makers of monuments (Göbel and Moog) in Düsseldorf, while waiting for opening of Düsseldorf Art Academy.

1948–   Studies sculpture and painting at Düsseldorf under Mages
1949   and Otto Pankok.

1951   Travel in Italy.

1952   Travel in France.

1953   Resumes studies at Berlin Art Academy as pupil of metal sculptor K. Hartung.

1954   Married to Swiss ballet dancer Anna Margaretha Schwarz. Wins third prize in poetry competition organized by South German Broadcasting Company. Travel in Spain.

1956   First exhibition of drawings in Stuttgart. *Die Vorzüge der Windhühner*. Moved to Paris.

1957   Exhibition of sculpture and drawings in Berlin. Premiere of first version of *Hochwasser* by Frankfurt students, January 21, and of the ballet *Stoffreste* in Essen (*Stadttheater*, choreographer; M. Luitpart).

1958   Receives stipend of "Kulturkreis der deutschen Industrie" and prize of "Gruppe 47" for chapter of *Die Blechtrommel*. Travel to Poland. Premiere of play *Onkel, Onkel* in Cologne.

1959 Became famous with publication of *Die Blechtrommel*. The Senate of the city of Bremen refuses to award literary prize for this novel. Three premieres: the ballet *Fünf Köche* (Aix-les-Bains and Bonn); the farce *Beritten hin und zurück* (Frankfurt student theater and "theater 53" in Hamburg); *Noch zehn Minuten bis Buffalo* (Schillertheater, Berlin).

1960 Berlin Critics' Prize for *Die Blechtrommel*. Grass finally moves to Berlin. *Gleisdreieck* published, with illustrations by the author.

1961 Story *Katz und Maus* published. Political activity: criticism of East German government at East Berlin Writers' Congress; open letter to East German writer Anna Seghers after building of Berlin Wall on August 13. *Die bösen Köche* published.

1962 Five-act play *Die bösen Köche* premiered (Schillertheater, Berlin). French award for *Die Blechtrommel*.

1963 Second long novel, *Hundejahre*, and revised version of play *Hochwasser* published. Elected to Academy of Arts, Berlin. Essay *Die Ballerina* published; second edition of *Vorzüge der Windhühner*.

1964 *Goldmäulchen* premiere in Munich. Shakespeare Year essay on "Coriolanus" published in *Akzente*.

1965 New version of *Onkel, Onkel* published. Independent election campaign with pamphlets for Socialist Party. Büchner Prize awarded by Darmstadt Academy.

1966 *Die Plebejer proben den Aufstand* premiered January 15 in Berlin and published. Journey to "Gruppe 47" meeting in Princeton, U.S.A.

1967 *Ausgefragt* published, with illustrations by the author.

Introduction

German Writers after the Second World War

In the concluding chapter of Thomas Mann's novel, *Doktor Faustus* (completed in 1947) the narrator, Serenus Zeitblom, regards with despair the pile of manuscript pages representing the completed account of the life of his friend, the composer Adrian Leverkühn. The year is 1945 and a devastated, guilt-laden Germany is plunging into the abyss of final ruin "in the grasp of demons," following the disastrous course already presaged in Leverkühn's life. Zeitblom wonders who will publish his work. Germany has been completely destroyed and its culture so thoroughly discredited "that one dare not hope that it might soon be capable of some cultural activity, even if only of the production of a book." Zeitblom considers the possibility of sending his manuscript to America, but rejects the notion, for he believes his work to be so characteristically German as to be untranslatable. In any case, he feels isolated from his fellow countrymen: "Germany itself, that ill-starred land, has become alien to me, dreadfully alien." The novel ends on a note of despair: "When will the light of hope dawn out of this utter hopelessness—a miracle that exceeds all belief?" [1]

The German situation in 1945 seemed indeed to justify description in apocalyptic categories. The very language had fallen into disrepute, and Walter Muschg, a Swiss literary historian, felt constrained to announce, even as he titled his book, "the destruction of German literature." [2] Yet, in fact, German literature proved to be a remarkably tough growth. In spite of Serenus Zeitblom's forebodings, *Doktor Faustus* was published (in Stockholm) in 1947, and an English translation appeared the following year.

Nor is *Doktor Faustus* an isolated case since it can be grouped with a number of novels of this period that make extensive use of myth and dream. Early postwar German novelists were strangely unanimous in choosing for their setting a mythical dream world in which they delineated their unassimilable present. Thus Elisabeth Langgässer, in *Das unauslöschliche Siegel* (1946), uses phantasmagoric visions to present the downfall of the existing order. The town which is the subject of Herman Kasack's *Die Stadt hinter dem Strom* (1947) is inhabited by the dead. Novels published by Ernst Kreuder and Stefan Andres in the late 1940's also fall into this category.

The visions of these authors, however, were too remote from grim reality to make any impact on the public. The first writer who treated World War II from the point of view of first hand experience —and the representative figure of the immediate postwar years— was Wolfgang Borchert. He had returned from the war in 1945, earlier than most of his fellow survivors, his health ruined by time spent in military prison and at the Russian front. Between 1945 and his death in 1947 he wrote both short stories and a play, *Draussen vor der Tür* (The Man Outside). His drama concerns the fate of a soldier, Beckmann, who limps home from Russia as "a ghost from the War." Beckmann is clearly a reflection of what Borchert felt to be his own situation. His play and his short stories are passionate cries of protest soon taken up by others, notably Hans Werner Richter and Heinrich Böll.

Various names were coined to designate the literature of protest against the war and its aftermath.[3] "Die Literatur der Obergefreiten" (Corporals' Literature) refers to the authors' attitude as being that of a resentful, low-ranking conscript. In *Kirschen der Freiheit* (Cherries of Freedom), for example, Alfred Andersch describes his desertion from the German army in Italy. Designation of this literature as "Heimkehrerliteratur" is a reference to the theme of the returning soldier; but the best-known term is "Trümmerliteratur" (Rubble Literature) because the setting was often a battle field or a bombed town. A typical short story by Borchert concerns a boy who keeps watch on the ruins of his bombed house under which his brother is buried; many of Böll's short stories are set in a makeshift world among the ruins of the late 1940's.

All these terms came to be used critically to imply distaste for the immediacy of perspective, the lack of detachment, or even the sentimentality of much early postwar writing—so much so that, in 1952, Böll felt obliged to defend "Trümmerliteratur," pointing out that in 1945 rubble was the only possible theme for any German writer.[4] The criticism, however, did not go unheeded. The fiction of Grass and other writers of the late 1950's is an attempt to achieve detachment without losing the authenticity of "Trümmerliteratur"; in other words, to assimilate recent history by rendering it in artistic terms. The pursuit of this aim is the history of that association of writers known as "Gruppe 47."

The Group has its roots in the postwar protest movement. In the beginning it was as much a political as a literary movement. Shortly after the war, to provide a platform for Borchert's "betrayed generation," H. W. Richter and Alfred Andersch, who had met as prisoners-of-war, founded a magazine, *Der Ruf.* One of the many periodicals that flourished briefly at that time, its tone displeased the American occupation authorities who, after sixteen issues, prohibited further publication. When a group of writers and journalists met in the Allgäu to found a new magazine to be called *Der Skorpion,* Richter had to inform the assembled company that permission to publish had been refused in advance. As a substitute for publication, the members read their manuscripts aloud and arranged to repeat the occasion a year hence. This gave rise to *Gruppe 47,* an annual meeting, still presided over by Richter, of authors and critics. Here the authors read aloud from their unpublished manuscripts and must then submit to impromptu, often ruthless criticism which they are expected to endure in silence. Some years the Group awards a prize to a newcomer whom they consider talented. From this loosely associated group, which claims to avoid all *isms,* programs and self-conscious *avant-garde,* many postwar German writers have emerged, although its importance is now said to be declining. By 1961, Walter Jens, Professor of Classics at the University of Tübingen, and an early member of *Gruppe 47* could include in his *Deutsche Literatur der Gegenwart* a list of over sixty reputable postwar writers, most of them associated with *Gruppe 47.*[5]

In emphasizing the part played by *Gruppe 47* in the revival of postwar German literature, Jens dates the real beginnings not from 1947, but from some years later. He even assigns an exact place and time to this fresh start, namely a meeting of *Gruppe 47* held in 1952, at which Paul Celan and Ingeborg Bachmann read their poetry and Ilse Aichinger (the prize-winner for that year) a short story, putting to shame the efforts of the "verists," the competent but uninspired storytellers who had preceded them.[6] In thus dramatizing the arrival of a new generation of writers, Jens was expressing his conviction that, until postwar writing had achieved detachment from the overwhelming events of the recent past, fiction would be the poor relation of factual reporting, properly left to the journalist and the historian. The days are past when a whole way of life could be captured by accurate reproduction, as Thomas Mann captured the era of the Lübeck patricians in *Buddenbrooks*. Artistic detachment must be based, however, on exact knowledge of the theme.

This striving for perspective and detachment, which Jens reports in 1952, only seven years after Germany's defeat, indicates the vitality of German postwar literature. Jens ruthlessly dismisses the stories and sketches of Borchert and the early Böll, and insists:

> No longer reports on concentration camps, but Celan's poem "Todesfuge" (Death Fugue) with its refrain "die schwarze Milch der Frühe" (the black milk of dawn); no longer "Trümmerliteratur" but symbol and image, Nossack's *Der jüngere Bruder* (The Younger Brother); no longer the soldier Beckmann returning from war, but Oskar, the drummer. The latter, not the former, is the embodiment of our times.[7]

CHAPTER 1

Günter Grass

GÜNTER Grass' first novel was *Die Blechtrommel* (The Tin Drum). Originally published in 1959, it won for Grass the 1958 prize of the *Gruppe 47*. Grass' novels are, indeed, good examples of the indirect approach which Jens commends as a method of rendering the modern scene.[1] In *Die Blechtrommel,* the author is apparently concerned with the inconsequential adventures of a mad dwarf, born in Grass' native Danzig, but now confined in a West German asylum. Grass' next novel, *Katz und Maus* (Cat and Mouse), published in 1961, is at first sight a preposterous story about a Danzig schoolboy who wears screwdrivers, medals and such around his neck to conceal a large Adam's-apple. The fall of the Third Reich in *Hundejahre* (Dog Years), published in 1963, is reflected in the adventures of a runaway dog. Grass is no isolated exemplar of this approach, for another member of the *Gruppe 47,* Wolfdietrich Schnurre in his 1959 novel *Das Los unserer Stadt* (The Fate of Our Town) does not describe the rain of bombs on Berlin and its subsequent occupation by conquering armies, but composes a surrealist vision of a town taken over by the forces of nature. Uwe Johnson's 1959 novel *Mutmassungen über Jakob* (Speculations about Jacob) does not give an account of life in Eastern Germany but is concerned with a highly speculative story about the private life of a railway worker. Johnson's next novel (1961), *Das dritte Buch über Achim* (The Third Book about Achim), elucidates the difference between a factual report and a novel; in a sense, this distinction is the very subject matter of Johnson's novel. The narrator of the work is a West German journalist who sets out to write a report on an East German racing cyclist, only to discover the impossibility of the task. Johnson's clear implication is that the novelist must not employ the straightforward account of events but must adopt what T. S. Eliot calls the "objective correlative." Grass finds this objective correlative in the grotesque—a literary development foreseen by Friedrich Schlegel in 1799 [2] and realized in the twentieth century by the Expressionists and the practitioners of the absurd theater. From both of these Grass borrowed extensively. Grass' employment of the grotesque often has pronounced elements of the obscene or the repulsive, for these are an essential part of his world, and closer inspection of one of his grotesque passages will serve as an introduction to Grass' methods.

One chapter of the second book of *Die Blechtrommel* bears the title "Brausepulver" (Lemonade Powder). Here Grass sets out, not from the characters involved, but from the very object itself, cheap lemonade powder, and he dwells on its characteristics with a wealth of verbs and adjectives that displays an exact knowledge of his humble subject:

Lemonade powder. Does that mean anything to you? Once it could be obtained throughout the year in little flat bags. In our shop, my mother sold little bags of woodruff-flavored powder of a sickly shade of green. One sort that had borrowed its color from oranges that were not quite ripe was called "Powder (Orange Flavor)."

Then there was powder with raspberry flavor and powder which, when plain water was poured on it, hissed, bubbled, became excited. When you drank it, before it calmed down, it tasted remotely and very faintly of lemon and had the same color in the glass, only somewhat more pronouncedly so: an artificial yellow that gave itself the air of being poison. (*Die Blechtrommel*, p. 330)

This effervescent, artificial powder plays an important part in the erotic passages involving the hero, Oskar, and Maria, the young shop assistant. They experiment and find that, poured into the palm of Maria's hand and brought to effervescence, it causes delicious, piquant sensations. The seething, tickling powder is an objective correlative of adolescent love and the clause "that had borrowed its color from oranges *that were not quite ripe*" is no mere random detail. It offers also an equivalent of the spirit of the 1930's (the setting in which the incident takes place) and that period's heady, dangerous enthusiasms: "when plain water was poured on it, [it] hissed, bubbled, became excited." The historical connotations clearly emerge when, in Western Germany after the War, Oskar attempts to buy lemonade powder, in the vain hope of recalling youthful ecstasies. An elderly shopkeeper informs him:

[14]

It's a long time since there was any of that about. Under Kaiser Wilhelm and, right at the beginning, under Adolf—then it was still sold. Those were the days! But if you'd like a Coca-Cola? (*Die Blechtrommel,* p. 345)

It requires no great critical astuteness to appreciate what Grass has done here, so subtly that many reviewers were at first deceived. Starting with the powder, Grass moves on to a human relationship and then, from this private sphere, to national conditions. Cheap lemonade powder, adolescent love in the 1930's and the Nazi movement are closely linked in a pattern of associations. Without argument, demonstration, protest or any display of enlightened anti-Fascist sentiment, the Nazi movement is placed firmly in an unmistakably *petit-bourgeois* context of cheap, fizzy chemical pop. Even the course of future developments and the relation of the past to the present is touched upon, briefly and without comment in the reference to the more sophisticated and distinctly postwar phenomenon of Coca-Cola.

The dominant role assigned to the artificial flavoring itself is characteristic. It is as if the whole world were controlled and regulated by that powder much as, in another episode, the crowd on the Danzig *Maiwiese* dances to the beat of Oskar's tin drum. The effect, similar to that of a sermon in which the preacher dwells on the correspondences and didactic aspects of a given text, is heightened by the baroque wealth of adjectives and the eccentric wit that recalls Johann Fischart or Abraham a Santa Clara.

In his brief portrait of Grass, Klaus Wagenbach notes the dominant part played by objects in Grass' fiction and characterizes this stylistic feature as "Objecktzwang" (compulsion through objects). The drum, for example, is especially dominant, particularly during the War. But even after the War, in the white-enamelled hospital ward of Western Germany its dictates stir Oskar to obedience. When he has completed a bizarre account of the death of Herbert Truczinski in the embrace of a wooden figurehead—another masterful object that embodies the disasters of Danzig's varied history—the attendant, Bruno, advises Oskar not to play so loudly in the future. Oskar promises that the next chapter will be more restrained. But the matter is out of his control. Shaman-like, he has drummed himself into a trance, so that the next chapter, dealing with the events of the "Kristallnacht," is the wildest of all. At the end of the First Book, the approaching war is heralded with a tattoo on the dominating drum—a series of sentences beginning with the childish, fairy-tale "Once upon a time. . ."

[15]

Wagenbach also observes that Grass' approach impels a neutral, amoral attitude on the part of the reader:

The objects are . . . so to speak, ruled by an object. In this way, no judgment is passed on an object by a subject; things keep themselves to themselves. It is hardly possible to consider such a text under the categories of disgust or delight, of the ugly or the beautiful.[3]

For all its grotesqueness, Grass' neutral approach eliminates certain distortions. Rolf Hochhuth, for example, in his play *Der Stellvertreter* (The Deputy), inadvertently lends his Nazi villains (e.g., the sinister, anonymous "Doktor" of Auschwitz) a spurious demonic grandeur which is lacking in Grass' object-dominated world. The arrival of the Russians in Danzig (*Die Blechtrommel*) is portrayed by the Party badge that Oskar's father has, until now, worn in his lapel. As in a music-hall sketch, he tries to hide the incriminating object, but the badge remains firmly in control and resists (with Oskar's help) all attempts to hide it. In desperation, Oskar's father tries to swallow it and chokes to death as Russian soldiers enter the cellar where he is sheltering with his family. This is Grass' highly unpathetic version of the end of the Third Reich.

Why does Grass place his reliance on objects? As he himself makes plain, moral, logical, and other man-made categories—seen in *Hundejahre* as a mere surrealist dance of scarecrows—are irrelevant to the actual course of events. Who can relate Hitler to the events linked with his name? Grass would never flatter Hitler in this way; instead, he allows a black dog to substitute for him. The brutal Stormtrooper Meyn in *Die Blechtrommel* is fond of his four cats, and a splendid trumpet player. The vicious Nazi girl, Tulla, who plays an important part in *Hundejahre* and appears in other novels as well, is permanently surrounded by a concentration-camp aura of bone-glue from the carpenter's yard where her father works. Yet she emerges as a figure of beguiling impulsiveness, while her victim Jenny, the gypsy girl, is kindly, shy and—apart from her dancing, dull and unenterprising. Combined, they would make a complete woman; but they stay apart—one to vanish in the postwar chaos in Danzig; the other to end her days behind the bar in a West Berlin beerhouse.

The main theme, to which Tulla and Jenny are a kind of counterpoint, is the relationship between Walter Matern and his partly Jewish blood-brother and school-friend, Eddi Amsel. Matern and eight other members of the SA ("Stormtroopers") beat up Amsel and leave him to die in the snow. The whole incident is wrapped in obscurity, yet this relationship is not simply that of persecuted and persecutor, but something far more ambiguous. Amsel has the firmer character, even though he is inclined to be physically flabby. Matern is, by descent, a moody Slav and vacillating—now a Communist, now a Nazi, now a Catholic, now violently and invariably opposed to all these persuasions. Closing his eyes to the guilt he incurred during the Nazi era, Matern travels about postwar Germany seeking revenge on former Nazis. His revenge, as impure as the cause, eventuates in the form of disseminating gonorrhea, so that Matern ends as the exhausted victim of his own vindictiveness.

Amsel, with his mocking talents, is resurrected as Haseloff, an international impresario and creator of a scarecrow ballet, and as Brauxel, whose underground scarecrow factories tunnel under affluent postwar Western Germany. To some extent, then, his talent for endurance, survival, and creation makes Amsel representative of the Spirit, while Matern stands for the Flesh. Strictly speaking, however, these categories do not fit very tightly since Matern has a serious, metaphysical bent, while Amsel is inclined to sensual indulgence. In short, although Grass denies to psychological complications and causality any ultimate importance in the shaping of events, he does not deprive his readers of the pleasures of character delineation.

The domination of the non-human over the human brings to mind the theater of the absurd. There, to compensate for the depreciation of human beings, objects often acquire a power which can at times become magical. For example, furniture takes control in Eugene Ionescu's *Le nouveau Locataire,* and chairs replace the guests in *Les Chaises.* True *chosisme* of this kind is characteristic of *Die Blechtrommel* and *Katz und Maus* rather than of *Hundejahre.* In the first of these two novels the drums and medals are the dictators. In *Hundejahre,* objects are replaced by scarecrows and dogs—animate, yet non-human—and the meaninglessness of human activities is directly demonstrated by means of the scarecrows that recur as a *leitmotif.*

Ironically it is Eddi Amsel, the victim of persecution, who is the master scarecrow builder. As a child, he constructs scarecrows, whose presence, frightening to birds, is finally anathema to people. During the war he creates mechanical scarecrows that enact the follies of Nazism and eventually becomes a worldwide supplier of scarecrows that are travesties of human history, theology, politics, social customs, normal and abnormal psychology—in fact, of every possible emotion and attitude. Imitated by scarecrows, human activities are seen as absurd, irrational, and empty of meaning, yet threatening and dangerous; for the artist is a blackbird (=Amsel), threatened by his own artifacts.

In *Hundejahre,* the dogs (which furnish the title of this work) provide a much stronger control over the situation than do the humans. "Der Hund steht zentral"—"the dog stands in the center"— is the running refrain. Harras and Prinz, sire and whelp, are descended from a Slav she-wolf. Harras starts life as a good, lower-middle-class watchdog, a typical German, dependable if somewhat rough in his ways. When Harras sires Prinz, who becomes Hitler's pet, he thereupon becomes a local celebrity and a bit of a Nazi. His sterling character shows a steady deterioration, however, and provides a comic analogy to the course of German history.

Grass' dominant "objects," whether inanimate or not, share the quality of moral indifference and ambiguity. Just as Oskar's drum is an equivalent of infantile dynamism, the dog is an equivalent of man's animality, an impartial force that can be used in various ways. The red and white colors of the drum are both German and Polish colors, and the dog is both a faithful hound and a Führer surrogate. It can be treated innocuously, or made into a scapegoat. Thus, when Prinz escapes, Hitler mobilizes his hard-pressed forces to recapture the emblematically German "Führerhund" (incidentally, the Allies, too, are interested). On another occasion, Matern, consumed by self-disgust at his own dalliance with the Catholic faith and the Nazi Party, curses Harras as "a black Catholic swine" (*Hundejahre,* p. 293).

This moral indifference is reinforced by a quality common in Expressionist writing, a quality which W. H. Sokel's analysis of the German Expressionist movement labels "extended metaphor." [4] Oskar's drum, Liebenau's dog, and the others leave the private sphere of the narrator's imagination, where they properly belong, and exert influence on the outside world. The people on the *Maiwiese* actually dance to Oskar's drum. Oskar's voice—another manifestation of his infantile dynamism—breaks actual windows (for which his mother has to pay), and the figurehead in the Danzig Museum actually causes deaths. The boundary between subject and object is eliminated, and the metaphor is, as Sokel puts it, "treated like an actual fact" with no reference to cause and meaning. Sokel takes as his example Kafka's celebrated salesman, Gregor Samsa, who is transformed into a beetle. Such extended metaphors can cover a wide range; Grass' scarecrows, the tin drum, and the others are broadly suggestive without being essential, defining, discrete and definitive. At their simplest and most amusing, Grass' objects translate a cliché or idiom into concrete form. The tin drum embodies the German idiom "Blech reden" (to talk nonsense); the "scarecrow" is a wretched-looking fellow; and so on.[5]

As in Laurence Sterne's *Tristam Shandy,* the uneasiness created by recalcitrant objects is reinforced by the peculiar behavior of time. In Grass' long novels, time varies its pace unpredictably. Sometimes it lingers, while at other times the narrative moves forward at a rattling pace. Again, there is a continual shift from past to present for the events of the narrative past are continually being compared with those of the narrator's present.

The opening chapters of *Die Blechtrommel* illustrate both these types of time manipulation. In spite of Oskar's claim that he is writing a straightforward, old-fashioned novel, the setting moves backwards and forwards between a cramped, hygienic ward in a postwar West German mental hospital and the former province of West Prussia where the narrator's grandparents lived in 1899. In the portrayal of the West German present, time lingers monotonously while Oskar ponders the purchase of five hundred sheets of writing paper; the past, as described, moves swiftly through time and space, from Kiev to Danzig, and involves a dramatic plot of love, crime, and violent death. The confrontation of the past with the present causes the reader to revise his views of the present—clean, confined, neurotic, and occupied with trivialities—whereas he regards the "provincial" past as earthy, yet full of far-ranging drama and a sense of history. Its uncramped security is objectified in the grandmother's skirt, a recurring motif in the novel.

More often, however, as Grass ranges to and fro in time, he views the Nazi era as part of history's flow. This is especially true of *Hundejahre,* which acquires its shape from the historical theme; the central story emerges from and ends in a welter of history. The novel opens on the banks of the Vistula, outside Danzig. Two boys are playing on the dikes: Eddi Amsel, partly Jewish, and his protector and potential persecutor, Walter Matern. As the river passes, it carries in its flow the rubble of a long history in which both boys will be involved. The panorama extends back to the Slav and Baltic gods of the region, the Teutonic Knights, Frederick the Great and the Princes of Pomerania. Myths and legends are included; one such concerns twelve headless nuns and twelve headless knights, and it recurs throughout the novel to transmit horror and violence from a chivalrous and sacred past into the present. The river dikes, however, are not dependable; they are infested with mice, and there is danger of flooding.

The main plot revolves about the flood that follows. It covers roughly the period of the Third Reich, which lasted about the lifetime of a dog. At the end of the novel we are brought back to the starting point. For the second time Matern throws Amsel's pocketknife into the river (this time not into the Vistula, but into the *Landwehrkanal* in Berlin) and insults his young Jewish friend. The story comes to rest in a mine near Hanover. There, Amsel, resurrected as Brauxel, manufactures scarecrows that enact a pageant of German and European history to bring the reader back to the opening theme.

The circular structure is not peculiar to *Hundejahre*. Grass' three novels place their narrators in postwar Germany, then proceed by narrowing the gap between the narrator's present and narrative time. But the journey has been made in vain because the traveler has really wandered around in a complete circle. Pilenz, in Western Germany, still fails to make contact with Mahlke. The thirty-year-old Oskar remains as childish as ever at the end of *Die Blechtrommel*. The refrain of the concluding nursery rhyme of the Black Cook, "Ist die schwarze Köchin da—ja, ja, ja," shows that terror continues to dominate his world. As one critic defines the situation: "Oskar takes leave of his readers, cites the shadow that has always been there and which will not leave him or us." [6]

The circular structure implies an attitude of criticism toward present-day Western Germany. The postwar Düsseldorf where Oskar settles bears a strong resemblance to the Nazi Danzig he has left; there is even a similarly eccentric character haunting the cemetery. The hero, Mahlke, remains absent from postwar Germany. In *Hundejahre*, the captains of industry are back in business. Yet Grass, for all his attacks on the Economic Miracle in the last book of *Hundejahre*, is not a satirist. He has none of that true satirist's indignation which betrays a belief that the world might possibly be set right. At bottom, Grass is expressing, by means of the circular structure of his novels, doubt whether progress is possible in human affairs, public or private. Here again, there is a parallel with the Theater of the Absurd: with Ionescu's *The Bald Soprano*, which ends with the opening phrases, or with Beckett's *Waiting for Godot*, where the tramps will presumably go on waiting.

Although Grass is not a satirist, he is a parodist. He uses parody as a means of further establishing an atmosphere in which everything is called into doubt. *Die Blechtrommel,* for example, is a parody of the *Entwicklungsroman,* the novel, of the type represented by Goethe's *Wilhelm Meister,* which gives an account of a young man's education until he reaches maturity. By using parody, Grass implicitly denies the optimism inherent in the genre. Oskar, its hero at an early stage of his life, takes a hard look at the world and decides to cease development at the age of three. His education includes the theatrical training that was an essential part of Wilhelm Meister's preparation for maturity, although in Oskar's case the theater consists of a touring troupe of midgets. Oskar's development reaches its peak in the grotesque pose he strikes as Jesus, a pose tacitly supported by his dubious claim to two fathers. A gang of young hooligans appoint him, in his role of Jesus, as their leader. Under his leadership they steal church furnishings during the last phase of the War. But it all comes to nothing. When the gang is caught, Oskar takes advantage of his outward appearance of a three-year-old boy to escape, abandoning his companions to their fate. The optimistic principles of the *Entwicklungsroman* clash with, and are defeated by, those principles of the absurd theater which reflect the inconclusiveness of life itself. The only development Oskar attains is a growth of some ten centimeters on the refugee train that takes him to the West. Even this modest result is achieved at the expense of his energy. Now a hunchback, Oskar can no longer shatter glass with his voice and is incapable of his adventures as a three-year-old—a mocking parallel to the development of the *Bundesrepublik* after the defeat of 1945.

The middle section of *Hundejahre* parodies the epistolary novel, of which the outstanding example in German literature is, of course, Goethe's *The Sorrows of Young Werther*. The *Hundejahre* parody takes the form of love letters written by Harry Liebenau to his cousin Tulla, an unchaste Lotte. The epistolary convention is treated with increasing perfunctoriness until it is finally abandoned and the letters are simply headed "Once upon a time."

Grass parodies not only genres, but also, in the manner of Joyce, individual authors. The kinship between Nazism and other currents of thought, which Thomas Mann's Serenus Zeitblom observes with horrified surprise, is suggested by means of parody, especially of Heidegger's language which abounds in *Hundejahre*. The messages sent to and from Hitler's Berlin bunker during the last days of the

War (when reality competed with the Theater of the Absurd) are progressively distorted until they become a strange mixture of military and philosophic jargon.

All Grass' novels parody the "Schelmenroman," the picaresque novel, in which, as Kayser[7] points out, the hero commonly ends his wandering life in a hermitage, in the manner of Grimmelshausen's *Simplicissimus*. This parodistic element is especially important in *Die Blechtrommel* in which Oskar, both hero and narrator, ends his days if not in a hermitage, in the cozy security of a sanatorium.

In placing the narrator in seclusion, Grass enables him to create a world in accordance with his own insane vision. Other authors have found this a convenient device. Max Frisch's *Stiller* speaks from a prison cell, and the narrator of Schnurre's *Das Los unserer Stadt* writes his chronicle in a monastery. Seclusion is a convincing method of enabling the narrator both to employ a variety of perspectives, ranging from that of participant to that of impartial judge, and to fuse realism with fantasy. Oskar takes full advantage of these possibilities, sometimes shifting from first to third person within a single sentence.

The wide range of Oskar's point of view is demonstrated at the very beginning of *Die Blechtrommel*. Oskar's simple-minded attendant, Bruno, regards his charge anxiously through a peephole, while the latter conjures up childhood memories on his drum. Uncertain, however, is whose point of view prevails at any given moment: Oskar's, "in front of" the peephole, or Bruno's, "behind" it? The matter is still further confused by Oskar's claim that he and his attendant are "both heroes, quite distinct heroes" (*Blechtrommel*, p. 12), although they are neither heroes nor distinct. The same range and uncertainty of viewpoint marks the opening of *Hundejahre*:

You tell the story. No, *you* tell it. Or you could tell it. Perhaps the actor should begin then? . . . Should the scarecrows all at once? . . . someone must begin. You or he or the other or I. (*Hundejahre*, p. 7)

Grass' wavering, contorted perspective owes its grotesque quality to the fact that it truthfully renders the situation of the novelist who is looking inward and outward simultaneously, recording his own impressions through the device of a narrator, and transforming them in doing so. What the novelist so records is personal, "a reflection of his individual intuition of the human situation," as Esslin[8] says of the Theater of the Absurd. The bizarre figures and situations, like those created by the Expressionists, which they sometimes closely resemble, appear to be dream figments.

The interpretation of the dream is left to the reader under the skillful guidance of the unseen author; the narrator in Grass' novels is not granted insight into the figures and events he describes. Oskar is seemingly unaware of the kinship that he and his drum bear to the childish aggressiveness of the outside world. If Amsel is aware that his scarecrows make fun of human activities, he is silent on that point. In matters of character interpretation, too, the author leaves much to the reader. For example, we must assume some kind of association between Meyn's action in killing his cats in *Die Blechtrommel* and his activities in the SA. When Herr Liebenau, the not very kindly carpenter, seizes an ax to smash Harras' kennel, we must assume that he has heard of Brunies' arrest and no longer supports the Nazi cause. Above all, *Katz und Maus* depends on the reader's having a deeper insight into Mahlke's heroism than is accorded to the narrator.

Every feature of Grass' works conspires to propagate uncertainty and the sense of a world deprived of meaning; yet doubt is not allowed to harden into a generally valid principle. One virtue which seems to be recommended by hint and implication can be circumscribed by such words as "unpretentiousness," "modesty," "atonement." It is often expressed by means of repulsive food. The play *Die bösen Köche* (The Wicked Cooks), for example, revolves around a cabbage soup made with ashes. Two rival factions of cooks are after the recipe, which turns out to be an incommunicable secret, yet a matter of living knowledge. The ashes of atonement recur in the poetry (e.g., "Der amtliche Tod" from *Gleisdreieck*) and in the novels. Mahlke in *Katz und Maus* demonstrates the unpretentious quality of his nature—which distinguishes his real heroism from the false heroism of his environment—by eating a can of frogs' legs salvaged from the wreck of a minesweeper lying in Danzig Bay.

In *Hundejahre*, Tulla's mourning for her deaf-and-dumb brother, the redeeming action of a ruthless character, takes the form of sharing with the dog repulsive offal from his bowl. (Characteristically, Grass describes the exact constituents of the stew and its preparation.) The death of Oskar's mother by fish-poisoning, seemingly deliberately induced after a Good Friday walk along the seafront near Danzig, is a kind of atonement for her lack of moderation, for her excessive love for Jan Bronski—a love which, itself, is expressed in terms of food: "My mother and Jan Bronski did not leave a single crumb. They ate everything up themselves. They have the appetite that never ceases" (*Blechtrommel*, p. 118). The sense of atonement as a necessary counterbalance to immoderation, and the association of this sense with repulsive food are most clearly expressed, as Wagenbach[9] was the first to point out, in a poem from *Gleisdreieck* entitled "Askese" (Asceticism). The speaker is a cat who recommends a sober, matter-of-fact manner of life in these terms:

> Du sollst, so spricht die Katze wieder,
> nur noch von Nieren, Milz und Leber,
> von atemloser saurer Lunge,
> vom Seich der Nieren, ungewässert,
> von alter Milz und zäher Leber,
> aus grauem Topf: so sollst du leben.

("Thou shalt, the cat went on to say, live only on kidneys, spleen and liver, on breathless, sour lung, on the urine from the kidneys, undiluted, on old spleen and tough liver from a gray pot: so shalt thou live.")

The cat broadly hints that part of this sobriety consists of dispensing with the excitement of war:

> Die Katze spricht.
> Was spricht die Katze denn?
> Du solltest die Marine streichen,
> die Kirschen, Mohn und Nasenbluten,
> auch jene Fahne sollst du streichen
> und Asche auf Geranien streun. (*Gleisdreieck*, p. 57)

("The cat speaks? What does the cat say? Thou shalt renounce the navy, cherries, poppy and nosebleed, strike those colors, too, and strew ashes on geraniums.")

The cat, it is to be observed, is not anxious, in the manner of, say, Heinrich Böll, to condemn militarism or martial glory as immoral or vicious; for the range of red objects which serve as ciphers for war extends from cherries, which are attractive, to bloody noses, which are painful and ludicrous. Nor does she make asceticism attractive (ashes on geraniums). Remaining neutral as to values, she recommends asceticism as a necessity. For Grass this necessary "asceticism" has one very concrete aspect, which emerges from his political addresses in which he repeatedly stresses the absolute renunciation of any ambition to regain the territories of which Germany was deprived after the war. Part of this unpalatable reality is plainly embodied in the food imagery, and it is greatly *ad rem* that Grass' childhood home is part of the lost territory.

Grass' permanent exile from Danzig (now the Polish city of Gdansk), coupled with the dilemma arising from this position, are central to his work. The exile remembers his lost home with astonishing accuracy. For all his bizarre distortions, which recall Expressionist visions, Grass has all the virtues of the old-fashioned novelist in the Naturalist tradition. He knows, and can render with meticulous accuracy, the appearance of a prewar elementary school, the life of a log rafter at the turn of the century, the work of a waiter in a dockside tavern, and how a grocer's shop was operated during the War. The variety of tones and dialects is equally impressive, and Grass is touchingly accurate in depicting the speech of *Skat* players (strangely neglected in German literature), of gypsies, minor Party officials, a patriotic schoolmaster exhorting his charges to be clean and hard. In this sense, Grass' fiction can be classified with that of a group of modern authors—Joyce, Faulkner, Pavese—whose works are bound up with a certain locality. Grass' very accuracy compels him to record such features of prewar Danzig as to make nostalgia absurd—the rise of the Nazis or the concentration camp near Stutthof (today Sztutowo), as examples. Yet the devices Grass uses to express his inevitable doubt and ambivalence, the visions and the parodies, are firmly rooted in a minutely observed *petit-bourgeois* background depicted down to the last potato dumpling.

On this combination of a doubting attitude and accuracy of detail Grass insists obliquely in the literary principle stated in his essay, "Inhalt als Widerstand" (Content as Resistance), published in *Akzente*.[10] In the first section of the essay, "A Distrustful Dialogue," Pempelfort and Krudewil, the eccentric railwaymen of *Noch zehn Minuten bis Buffalo*, are now more congenially employed as poets. Krudewil rejects his companion's ecstasies over flowers and sits down to knit a new, matter-of-fact Muse: "Our new Muse is a skilled housewife. A faulty upper part would annoy her. She would dismiss us ruthlessly, have herself unwound and re-knitted on a machine." In the final section of this essay, Grass uses an illustration from cooking to demonstrate the need to beware of falsity of tone. "Where eggs are served as soft-boiled, it is best to convince oneself with the spoon," he cryptically observes. The vigilance has the purpose of ensuring that the poet remain close to the object and not depart from it to make sweeping generalizations. Grass assumes that the poet will choose a close-mesh wire fence as subject; a bad poet will rave enthusiastically: "The cosmos must be included, the motor elements of the meshed wire should swell to supertemporal, supersensual staccato, completely dissolved and fused into a new system of values." He would be better advised, says Grass, to stay with the original wire fence as supplied by Lerm and Ludewig, Berlin.

These principles work best in Grass' novels on which his reputation so far rests. In his poetry, the grotesque images, divorced from the exactly observed associative environment, often seem mere surrealistic trifling. Grass' absurd plays are accounted imaginative but slight, yet his latest political play, *Die Plebejer proben den Aufstand* (The Plebeians Rehearse the Uprising), suffers from lack of dramatic development. In the novel, however, Danzig, lost to Germany politically, finds a place in German literature.

CHAPTER 2

Grass' Poetry

GRASS made his first, unobtrusive entry onto the literary scene with a sixty-page volume of poems and short prose passages published in 1956 under the strange title, *Die Vorzüge der Windhühner*.[1] The windfowl are the airy creations of Grass' imagination depicted on the front cover, and their good points (*Vorzüge*) are dwelt on in an introductory poem printed on the flap. The poet makes no great claims for his creations, but he shyly recommends them to the reader:

> Weil sie kaum Platz einnehmen
> auf ihrer Stange aus Zugluft.

("Because they take up hardly any room on their perch made of air-currents.")

Initially, Grass studied modeling and drawing at the Düsseldorf Academy of Art under the sculptor Sepp Mages and the painter Otto Pankok, both of whom are caricatured in *Die Blechtrommel* as Maruhn and Kuchen. On his return from visits to France and Italy, he continued his studies at the Berlin Academy of Art in 1953. One of his poems was allegedly shown to Gottfried Benn in Berlin, and although Benn found it promising, he advised its author to try his hand at prose. Grass married in 1954 and the story is that his wife entered one of his poems for a 1955 competition conducted by the South German Broadcasting Company in Stuttgart.[2] Grass' poem won the third prize and was published in the bi-monthly literary magazine *Akzente*.[3] Grass soon began to publish regularly in *Akzente*.

As a result of his modest success in the poetry competition, the unknown Grass received an invitation to a meeting of the *Gruppe 47*, and this, in turn, led to the acceptance of his first volume of verse by a publisher. Grass' drawings, which appear in the three volumes of verse so far published, reflect and reinforce the poetry itself, for in both drawings and poetry there is a threat lurking under the apparently infantile surface doodling.[4] Insects are a favorite motif in *Die Vorzüge der Windhühner*—a dying spider trapped in a glass; a design formed of insect legs and heads illustrates the poem "Die Mückenplage" (The Plague of Midges); and he has made a point with his drawing of a locust invading a town, a beetle on its back, disintegrating. Even the "windfowl" on the front cover, with their stiltlike legs, look like insects, although the weird, twisted manner in which they stretch their necks shows that they are made of paper.

The introductory poem mentions only the childlike, unforced nature of the "windfowl": "Oft bei Ostwind . . . lehne ich glücklich am Zaun/ ohne die Hühner zählen zu müssen,—weil sie zahllos sind und sich ständig vermehren" (Often when the East wind blows, I lean happily on the fence without having to count the windfowl— because they are innumerable and increase steadily). The East wind in this quotation blows from Danzig to inspire Grass' poetry with the breath of childhood memories. In "Die Klingel" the act of composition is identified with that of recollection: "Weil die Erinnerung sich stückeln lässt und längen,/ so eine Katze unter Streicheln" (as memory can be cut up and stretched like a cat when it's stroked). The real subject of this and related poems, however, is the threat to the childhood world because the windfowl are not so carefree as they pretend. Thus "Bohnen und Birnen" (Beans and Pears) takes its title from a popular North German dish of the poet's childhood, usually eaten in summer. This reminds Grass not of summer, however, but of the approaching autumn, when spiders take refuge from the cold air. The threatened childhood is also the theme of "Blechmusik" (Brass Band), where birth is seen as the emergence from a trumpet, as it is at the beginning of the play *Die bösen Köche* (The Wicked Cooks):

> Damals schliefen wir in einer Trompete.
> Es war sehr still dort,
> wir träumten von keinem Signal,
> lagen, wie zum Beweis,
> mit offenem Mund in der Schlucht,—
> damals, ehe wir ausgestossen.

("In those days we slept in a trumpet. It was very quiet there, we dreamed of no signal, we lay, as if to prove this, with open mouths in the abyss—in those days, before we were expelled.")

The next stanza asks who woke us from our childhood dream and it proposes three possibilities: a child "with a helmet on his head made of old newspaper"; a mad hussar; Death himself. The child with the paper hat, familiar from Grass' own cover design for *Die Blechtrommel*, appears here as a generalized cipher of destruction, death, and shattered childhood peace.

In Grass' novels, the destruction of Danzig specifically represents the loss of childhood. In his poetry the threat to the childhood world is conveyed in less specific terms. A further example is found in the group of five poems—"Messer, Gabel, Scher' und Licht"— based on a couplet for German children which cautions against playing with knives, forks, scissors, and fire. In Grass' absurd adaptation of this rhyme, the scissors are seen as a kind of woman that can "do the splits" and inflict pain. The transition from childhood to adolescence is represented by means of a girl who, ignoring all warnings, swallows a fork which "burns, two lots of five fingers," and brings further disasters in its train. Scissors are aroused to cut off girlish plaits and stir up serpents. The hair that is cut off strangles the dolls of childhood.

The doll is one of the inhabitants of the world of Grass' poetry, a disturbingly helpless victim of aggressive impulses. Thus in "Lamento bei Glatteis" (Lament in Icy Weather), the doll Sana is cut open and the sawdust scattered on the ice, in spite of the poet's anxiety that she should remain intact in preparation for a kinder season. In "K, der Käfer," the helplessness of the beetle (*Käfer*) as it lies on its back, recalls other K's—Kafka and the dolls designed by the famous German puppet-maker, Käte Kruse.

Gleisdreieck, Grass' second volume of verse, contains two full-page charcoal drawings of dismembered dolls. Accompanying these is a group of four-lined, unrhymed verses, "Aus dem Alltag der Puppe Nana" (From the Daily Life of the Doll Nana), representing the doll in situations that induce bewilderment and fear.

Birds, another recurring cipher, are associated with the sources of Grass' poetry. The association is cryptically conveyed in the first poem of *Die Vorzüge der Windhühner* with the title "Vogelflug" (Flight of Birds). The flight which the poem celebrates takes place in the imagination: "Über meiner linken Braue/ liegt Start und Ziel/ für immer begründet" (Over my left brow start and finish are fixed forever). The source of poetry, then, is memory—the realm of Mnemosyne. To be able to exploit his memory, the poet is represented as resolving to return later, when the swallows have departed, so that he can fly a piece of paper like a kite. The poet is shown also raising his arm to keep the flight of birds at arm's length. Light is thrown on this mysterious statement in the prose passage "Fünf Vögel" (Five Birds). There, in the course of some extended trifling with various fancies, the five birds, subject of this passage, emerge as identical with the poet's fingers. A drawing of the five birds show that they are very similar to the paper "windfowl" on the title page. The poetry, then, is contrived by the poet out of his own resources, so to speak, as the fruits of reminiscence and reflection. In a later poem, "V, der Vogel," the birds become threatening. The letter "V" for "Vogel" (bird) and for five fingers becomes a wedge "to split a heaven."

The dolls and birds, scarecrows and nuns of Grass' poetry are hints at motifs that are more fully developed in the novels. In his poetry, especially in the earlier verse, the effect is of purely personal imagery; thus "Musik im Freien" (Music in the Open Air):

> Als der gelbe Hund über die Wiese lief
> verendete das Konzert.
> Später fand man den Knochen nicht mehr.
> Die Noten lagen unter den Stühlen,
> der Kapellmeister nahm sein Luftgewehr
> und erschoss alle Amseln.

("When the yellow dog ran across the meadow, the concert died miserably. Later the bone was no longer to be found. The notes lay under the chairs. The conductor took his airgun and shot all blackbirds.")

Readers of *Hundejahre* will recognize the attempt to find an equivalent for terror in images that are at once familiar and bizarre. Similarly, particles of the mythology of *Die Blechtrommel* are dimly visible in the three poems "Drei Vater Unser" (Three Paternosters). The opening address to "Power," for example, endows this entity with the ability to shatter glass with its voice, like Oskar, and goes on to associate this dynamism with the urge to make war:

> Kommen einfach her,
> zersingen die Gläser

>   und wollen noch Beifall.
>   Mars, böse Metzger bestimmen die Preise.

("[You] simply come here, shatter the glasses by singing and want applause, too. Mars, wicked butchers decide the prices.")

Similarly, "Hochwasser" (Flood) is a preliminary sketch to the play of the same name. Both poem and play mention the checking of packing cases brought up from the cellar and the sewing of sunshades even as the catastrophe is at its height. The play amusingly indicates that the catastrophe and its effects are not always wholly unwelcome. The poem ends with a delicate hint at the same idea: "We shall often go down into the cellar to look at the mark that the water left behind."

Actually, Grass is sometimes so spare in his methods, so anxious not to allow comparison to intervene between content and poetic statement that the interpreter of his poetry cannot resist turning to his explicit prose passages to check or confirm the clues he has gathered from the poetry itself. "Die bösen Schuhe" (The Wicked Shoes) begins:

>   Die Schönheit steht—
>   und oben im Applaus
>   gerinnt das Lächeln, Milch
>   in blossen Schalen. . .

("Beauty stands—and at the top, in the midst of applause, the smile curdles, milk in uncovered dishes.")

At the end of the second stanza, a single word reveals that the shoes of the title are worn by a ballerina:

>   . . . —die Schönheit dauert
>   in spitzen Schuhen, relevé.

("Beauty endures in pointed shoes, relevé.")

From Grass' essay, "Die Ballerina" we know of the importance he attributes to the fact that the ballerina acquires her disciplined art at the expense of torturing her feet in unnatural shoes with toe-blocks.[5] The foundation of her grace and beauty, the essay states, is the hours of patient practice before a mirror, to say nothing of her misshapen feet. For one who has read the essay, with its explicit contrast between the ballerina's art and the foundations on which it is built, the fragmentary hints of the poem fall easily into place. Grass' poetry, however, has avoided posing obvious rhetorical contrasts; his method is rather to scatter hints and fragments of thoughts and images. He wants to avoid the mistake of the other dancer whom he describes in his essay, the opposite number and deadly enemy of the ballerina. This dancer endeavors to express her soul "as if her private and, moreover, bent knee were reason enough to enthrall one-eighth of the stalls and the half-filled balcony." Because Grass, too, has taken pains in his poetry to avoid demonstrative posing, the result is that his poetic statements are all too often tight-lipped and cryptic.

"Bohnen und Birnen" is an exception, and so is "Polnische Fahne," a poem which dwells on the theme of Polish gallantry exemplified in Marshal Pilsudski's campaign against the Russians in 1920. For this subject Grass evidently feels that a touch of rhetoric and theatricality is not out of place. The poem employs the associations aroused by red and white, the colors of the Polish flag. While the red is, of course, blood, the poem opens with cherries as a derivative of this blood, something more than the merely martial that makes the bloody aspect acceptable. The poem proceeds in pictures of frost and fire to reach a rhetorical, alliterative climax in:

> Pilsudskis Herz, des Pferdes fünfter Huf,
> schlug an die Scheune bis der Starost kam.

("Pilsudski's heart, the horse's fifth hoof, beat on the barn until the starost came.")

Only on occasions are the windfowl as carefree as their creator claims. Even such pieces of nonsense verse as "Schule der Tenöre" (School for Tenors) strike a warning note. Social criticism is not entirely suppressed. "Prophetenkost" (Prophets' Fare) tells of a town, invaded by locusts, that releases its prophets from jail—until the plague has passed. The third of the three "Vater Unser" directs a preacher's warning against the postwar world and employs a simile strange to Grass' poetry:

> Ihr solltet nicht mehr die Ratten impfen,
> Ratten rächen sich,

[32]

knabbern an Fundamenten,
suchen die Toten heim,—
wie der Tod euch   ,
mit Fernsehen heimgesucht hat.

("Ye shall no longer innoculate rats, for rats take their revenge, gnaw at foundations, haunt the homes of the dead—just as Death haunts your home with television.")

The poem "Warnung" (Warning) is far more circumspect in its generalized admonition, "Vorsicht, der Wind schläft in Tüten" ("Be careful—the wind sleeps in paper bags"). In the five-line "Familiär," Grass employs the grotesque cipher:

Unsere abgetriebenen Kinder, blasse, ernsthafte Embryos,
sitzen dort in schlichten Gläsern
und sorgen sich um die Zukunft ihrer Eltern.

("Our aborted children, pale, earnest embryos, sit there in simple jars and worry about their parents' future.")

The underlying idea that the deliberate distortion and destructiveness of the present kills all future hopes is part of the total pattern of Grass' novels. Examples of this are found in the self-inflicted deformity of Oskar, the suppression of the true hero in *Katz und Maus*, and the miscarriage scene in *Hundejahre*.

The calm, reflective mood in which the poet leans on the fence to watch the windfowl plays its part, too, in creating the total impact. The poet's "Credo" begins with "Mein Zimmer ist windstill" ("In my room there is a lull") and ends with "Niemals werden wir stranden" ("We shall never founder"). The same calm reigns in "Rundgang" (Going the Rounds) where, as in the "Creed," the wallpaper and the domestic objects emphasize, by their suggestion of storms elsewhere, the calm that surrounds the reflective poet. The planets as well as the policemen, postmen, and foresters go their rounds sheltered from storms. "Die Klingel" (The Doorbell) similarly finds the poet in his room "half awake in the thicket of curtains," attempting to utilize his recollections for poetry:

Versuche mit Tinte
Niederschriften im Rauch.

("[I] try with ink to write in smoke.")

The situation of the room where the poet loses himself in reflection and the act of composition is indicated in "Das endlose Laken" (The Endless Sheet). In his right ear the poet can hear sounds from the Berlin railway junction Gleisdreieck, where, before the Communists built the wall, the trains connecting East and West arrived and departed. At this point was concentrated the threat represented by a divided Berlin, a source of crises since the end of the War. This threat, which infests the whole city, is transferred to an object—to the apparently harmless bedsheet which turns into a strangling monster.

This particular threat so impressed Grass that he titled his second volume of verse, *Gleisdreieck*.[6] The work was published in 1960 after the recognition accorded *Die Blechtrommel*. Two drawings of a giant spider brooding over a hazily indicated stretch of railway reveal his recognition of the threat inherent in the dread landmark. The title poem, fourth in the collection, explains the spider as an embodiment of Gleisdreieck:

> Gleisdreieck, wo mit heisser Drüse
> die Spinne, die die Gleise legt,
> sich Wohnung nahm und Gleise legt.

("Gleisdreieck, where with hot spinner the spider that lays rails took up residence and lays rails.")

The first verse conveys the uncertainty and agitation of a divided city:

> Die Putzfraun ziehen von Ost nach West.
> Nein, Mann, bleib hier, was willst du drüben;
> kommrüber, Mann, was willst du hier.

("The charwomen move from East to West. No, husband, stay here, what do you want over there; come over here, husband, what do you want here.")

Two other poems of this collection are concerned with the Berlin theme. The first, "Brandmauern," takes its name from the "firewalls" between tenement houses. In many districts of Berlin only these firewalls remained standing after 1945, and they were still a characteristic feature of the Berlin landscape when Grass moved there in 1960.

The poem (and the whole volume) opens with a magic formula to placate the spirit of the place:

> Ich grüsse dich Berlin, indem ich
> dreimal meine Stirn an eine
> der Brandmauern dreimal schlage.

("I greet you, Berlin, by beating my forehead three times against one of the firewalls.")

But the spirit remains unplacated; for in the penultimate poem Grass presents a *genius loci* in the form of a giantess who presides over the rubble of the ruined city. A crude, childish drawing shows this "Trümmerfrau" sitting amidst the debris, hammering a brick to dust. She sings her lament, each of whose twenty-three strophes begins as if with hammerblows. As this giantess crushes the ornamental masonry of Kaiser Wilhelm's Berlin, the frail new buildings tremble at the constant reminder of the recent holocaust. Her lament is heard all over the city, but radio stations, East and West, pretending not to hear it, broadcast interminable waltzes. The giantess, however, will not be ignored and she forces Berliners to swallow the soup of atonement:

> Tot ist sie tot
> sagen die Baumeister,
> verschweigen aber, dass eine unabwendbare Hand
> Mittag für Mittag löffelweis toten Mörtel
> in ihre Suppe mengt.

("Dead, she is dead, say the builders, but do not mention that, every noon, a remorseless hand mixes dead mortar into their soup by the spoonful.")

The "Trümmerfrau" ogress is one of many similar figures from Grass' private mythology which embody the cruelty of the world in the form of a fairy tale. In fact, the whole volume demonstrates this "dialectic" process. Its format, with oversize pages and print, thick paper and scrawls that wastefully occupy entire pages and even double pages (for example, the grinning nuns spread across pages 46 and 47 and pages 52 and 53), is deliberately infantile. The underlying facts, however, are harsh and real.

The contrasting worlds are central to the second poem of the collection, "Adebar." The title, name of the stork in North and East German folklore, means "bringer of luck." The stork builds its nest on smokeless chimneys and brings children to the house. From here the poem moves, by association, to the crematorium chimneys of the extermination camp of Treblinka, in Poland, so that unequalled historical reality is accentuated by the poetic context:

> Einst rauchte in Treblinka sonntags
> viel Fleisch, das Adebar gesegnet,
> liess, Heissluft, einen Segelflieger steigen.

("Once there smoked in Treblinka on Sundays flesh that Adebar had blessed, hot air to fly a glider.")

The concrete historical instance is not necessary to Grass' poetry; in "Kinderlied" (Nursery Rhyme), as an instance, the rocking rhythm is childish, while the speaker's warning contains the harsh threat that there is nothing to laugh at:

> Wer hier stirbt, unverdorben
> ist ohne Grund verstorben.

("Whoever dies here unspoilt has died in vain.")

The dialectic relationship between historical fact and infantile fantasy, explored in these poems, is one of the threads running through *Die Blechtrommel. Gleisdreieck* contains a number of less successful poems which are variations of themes encountered in the novel. The bunker on the invasion beach in Normandy reappears with a former officer (here a general) sentimentally stroking the embrasures. In the poem "Zauberei mit den Bräuten Christi' (Magic with Christ's Betrothed) the nuns of *Die Blechtrommel* reappear on the beach with their umbrellas. As in the novel, the nuns are transformed into sailing ships, to avenge the earlier naval victories of the Protestant English.

A short poem, "Der Dichter" (The Poet), takes up another motif from *Die Blechtrommel,* that of the German script "Sütterlinschrift" taught to German children from 1915 until about 1940. The poem begins cryptically by calling the "Sütterlinschrift" evil, then goes on to relate how rabbits die when children tell them of it. In the novel, Oskar in his very first day at school encounters letters in this script.

Its slings and hangman's nooses cause him to think of the hand-written death warrants of the Nazi era. What is puzzling in the poem appears in the novel as an indication of evil lurking in a child-hood idyll. The scarecrows in "Die Vogelscheuchen" (The Scare-crows) are merely bewildering, without the associative framework of *Hundejahre,* even though the poem is accompanied by two double-page scrawls.

In this second volume of poetry, however, Grass is more willing than in the first to use readily comprehensible images and associa-tions and a clear metric and strophic form. "Kirschen" (Cherries), for example, imagines true love on stilts, picking cherries with ele-gance and ease, while the poor poet must struggle with an inade-quate ladder and be satisfied with windfalls. In "Klappstühle" (Folding Chairs) the elaborate patent folding chairs found aboard steamers, "laden with homesickness and queasiness," are appropri-ately associated with impermanence. "Saturn" renders the gloom of solitary lodgings; the presiding deity, for example, cleans his teeth with cigarette ash. "Pan Kiehot," on the familiar theme of Polish gallantry, depicts the Polish Don Quixote attacking German tanks near Kutno, as the Polish cavalry did in 1939.

"Falada," the name of the horse whose severed head speaks to reveal the identity of the true princess in Grimm's savage fairy tale "The Goose-girl," employs images from a butcher's shop, just as "Annabel Lee" (subtitled Hommage à E. A. Poe) plays with pictures of decay and with rhymes. Further graveyard humor occurs in "Geflügel auf dem Zentralfriedhof" (Hens in the Cemetery); here the serious bearing of the hens that scratch about in the cemetery contradicts the German idiomatic phrase "da lachen ja die Hühner" —"it's enough to make the hens laugh."

One poem, "Goethe" belongs to a type that will be more frequently met with in *Ausgefragt.* It observes the poet's domestic life with mild satire and a touch of anxiety. "Goethe" displays a certain dislike of the members of the literary "establishment" who visit the poet and discuss books in gentle cultured tones while eyeing his wife. Grass apparently sees himself as neither gentle nor cultured, but as one who crudely strives for honesty. This is emphasized in "Diana—oder die Gegenstände" (Diana or the Objects), a poem in *Gleisdreieck* which comes close to being a statement of artistic principle. Diana, the poets' Muse—illustrated as a huge misshapen woman sprawling over two pages—shoots with an object at the poet's soul which, to her, is also an object. Objects must dominate because ideas are insubstantial:

> Immer lehne ich ab
> von einer schattenlosen Idee
> meinen schattenwerfenden Körper verletzen zu lassen.

("I always refuse to let my body, which casts a shadow, be injured by a shadowless idea.")

The attachment to objects as a mode of viewing the world leads Grass to give the title "Inventar" (Inventory) to a poem which depicts a domestic quarrel through a succession of broken or displaced objects. "Der Vater" (The Father) is a simple demonstration of the power to embrace the paradox of a common situation that emanates from objects. Household utensils this time serve to demonstrate not only the father's authority but also his helplessness. When fuses blow or there is a knocking in the pipes, the children reproachfully look at him because he is all-powerful and, therefore, responsible.

"Der Vater" touches on the question of the guilt of the older generation, a question which is rarely far from the surface in Grass' work. A number of poems in *Gleisdreieck* are concerned with this guilt. As in "Askese," mentioned in Chapter 2, Grass reinforces his invitation to his fellow countrymen to eliminate pageantry and pride in the poem "Kleine Aufforderung zum grossen Mundaufmachen— oder der Wasserspeier spricht" (A Brief Invitation to Open the Mouth Wide—or the Gargoyle Speaks). In what are almost preacher's tones, Grass asks the older generation to make a clean breast of it and to release the foulness that lurks "behind the toothpaste":

> Wir wollen nun den Mund aufmachen
> die schlimmen Goldzähne,
> die wir den Toten brachen und pflückten,
> auf Ämtern abliefern.

("Let us now open our mouths and hand over to the authorities the bad gold teeth that we broke and plucked from the dead.")

"Im Ei" (In the Egg) depicts human life as a matter of cramped quarters decorated, like Oskar's cell, with improper drawings. If the cultivation of the inner life is thus ironically observed, so is the optimistic expectation that some beneficent being will preside over the hatching of the egg. Above all, any immodest Nietzschean urge to philosophize with the hammer is dealt with in the final strophe:

> Wenn wir auch nur noch vom Brüten reden,
> bleibt doch zu befürchten, dass jemand,
> ausserhalb unserer Schale, Hunger verspürt,
> uns in die Pfanne haut und mit Salz bestreut.—
> Was machen wir dann, ihr Brüder im Ei?

("Even if we merely talk about hatching, it is to be feared that some-one outside our shell will feel hunger, dash us into the frying pan and sprinkle us with salt. What shall we do then, o brothers in the egg?")

With the smashing of the egg, Grass is on the familiar territory of modern poetry, inhabited by nameless chimeras that lurk behind the thin veil of perceived reality. Grass' fragmentary images and the deliberate flouting of logical development underline the resemblance to his contemporaries and his descent from the writers of nonsense verse—Morgenstern, Ringelnatz, and Hans Arp. The language of this poetry is hard, unfeeling, metallic, and lacking in immediate emotional appeal. Marie Luise Kaschnitz describes it:

> Die Sprache, die einmal ausschwang,
> > Dich zu loben,
> Ziehr sich zusammen, singt nicht mehr
> > In unserem Essigmund.[7]

("Language which once soared to praise Thee, now contracts [and] sings no more in our vinegar mouths.")

At times, however, Grass' verse does "sing." The childhood theme seems to occasion these bursts of traditional lyricism. Describing the street organs that used to appear at the beginning of spring, "Dreh-orgeln kurz vor Ostern" (in *Die Vorzüge der Windhühner*) con-jures up an image of endangered childhood:

> Drehorgeln
> immer zu früh grünende Herzen.

("Hurdygurdies—hearts that always grow green too soon.")

On September 21, 1965, the weekly newspaper *Die Zeit* published a poem in which Grass allowed himself the luxury of writing about his childhood in evocative, rhythmical verse. In this issue three German authors wrote about their birthplaces; Grass' contribution was a poem of ten iambic stanzas on Danzig. He chose the title "Kleckerburg," a reference to the castles built with wet sand on the beaches of the Baltic coast:

> Hier, wo ich meine ersten Schuhe
> zerlief, und als ich sprechen konnte,
> das Stottern lernte: Sand klatschnass,
> zum Kleckern, bis mein Kinder-Gral
> sich gotisch türmte und zerfiel.
> Das war knapp zwanzig Jahre nach Verdun. . .

("Here, where I wore out my first shoes and, when I could talk, learned to stutter: sand, dripping wet to make it stick until my childish grail towered Gothic and crumbled. That was a bare twenty years after the battle of Verdun. . .")

In this atmosphere of heartfelt lyricism and personal reminiscence, some of Grass' ciphers (e.g., the lemonade powder of *Die Blechtrommel,* the pocket-knife of *Hundejahre*), appear as symbols of his Danzig years, recalled in Western Germany:

> Geboren wann? und wo? warum?
> Das hab ich hin und her geschleppt,
> im Rhein versenkt, bei Hildesheim begraben
> doch Taucher fanden und mit Förderkörben
> kam Strandgut Rollgut hoch, ans Licht.
> Bucheckern, Bernstein, Brausepulver,
> dies Taschenmesser und dies Abziehbild,
> ein Stück vom Stück, Tonnagezahlen,
> Minutenzeiger, Knöpfe, Münzen,
> für jeden Platz ein Tütchen Wind.

("Born when? and where? and why? I have trailed that about, sunk it in the Rhine, buried it near Hildesheim, but divers found it, and flotsam and jetsam was dredged up. Beechnuts, amber, lemonade powder, this pocket-knife and this transfer picture, a piece of a piece, tonnages, minute-hands, buttons, coins, a bag of wind for every place.")

[40]

Grass included this poem in his third volume *Ausgefragt* [8] (Questioned). In this same volume are two poems "Ja" (Yes) and "Schreiben" (Writing) in which he reveals something of his aims and methods. "Ja" raises the problem that every positive statement bears within it its own contradiction. Grass, who adduces the widow's "no" as a ribald example, implies that his aim is to find the gray, intermediate notes that fret between black and white; or, in another image, to use the third exit to a house with two exits. This admission of distrust toward definite statements explains many of Grass' characteristic techniques. The truncated phraseology of "Kleckerburg" (It was once called so today called so/ There lived there till, from then on lived) leaves open the question as to whether the poet is too indifferent or too griefstricken to complete his statement about the subsequent fate of Danzig.

As he states it in "Schreiben," Grass' aim is to convey the imprecise precisely ("das Ungenaue genau treffen"). In pursuit of this aim, he follows Benn in insisting on the direct statement of poetic vision, without the intercession of comparison or simile: "because . . . on account of . . . as . . . so that . . . so as to . . . similes and that kind of all-purpose glue." In the same way Benn condemns the simile as "a weakness of the creative transformation." [9] Where the poetry renders the very substance of reality, the reader will not have to be impatient; he will have to "remain cheerful in the vacuum." Thus Grass concludes "Schreiben" with a colon and the assurance "I shall come back."

Grass' method in these latest poems remains that of the collector of everyday objects and, increasingly, of everyday phrases. His poetry is the "Lost Property Office" mentioned in "Schreiben." In "Schlager im Ohr" he "collects noises and pins them to the wall." Without difficulty the reader of *Hundejahre* can place these sounds —"my grandfather's circular saw," air-raid warnings, heavy bombs exploding, and brewery horses on cobbled streets. In "Advent" these reminiscences of the thirties and forties are replaced by modern objects and phrases. The nursery, represented by Donald Duck, has little difficulty in blending with the world of great events, represented by current jargon—"escalation," "conventional warfare," and the rest. There are also purely political poems, such as "Neue Mystik," describing a new hodgepodge religion as "a meeting of Spiritualist Leninists in Lourdes."

For the most part, however, Grass is content to let his objects speak for themselves. In accordance with the principle expressed in

"Ja" ("everything beautiful is crooked"), he shows a strong preference for homely objects, often such kitchen objects as canned vegetables in "Gemüsetest" (Vegetable Test), cooked fish in "Bei Tisch" (At Table), a garbage disposal in "Schreiben." "Schweinskopfsülze" is almost entirely a lengthy account (not to be recommended for people with delicate stomachs) of the preparation of *Sülze*, or brawn, from a pig's head. The whole process allegedly aids the cook in ridding himself of stored-up rage, while providing his family with a cheap and nourishing dish. "Ehe" (Marriage) is, in effect, an assembly of stock phrases from which a marriage, in all its ambiguity, can be discerned in an outline that is at once bizarre and real.

The poems in this collection are, for the most part, more genuinely casual than those of the earlier volumes and frequently concern domestic or private life. Thus a visit to the United States occasioned the poem "Badeleben" (Bathing Scene): "Budweiser's cans" which litter the beach help provide local color. There are frequent references to the Vietnam war, and the election poem "Gesamtdeutscher März" (Pan-German March) is reprinted here; but there is also a group of verses, "Zorn Ärger Wut" (Wrath Anger Rage), which deal half-humorously with the futility of protest.

CHAPTER 3

Grass and the Theater of the Absurd

THE transition from poetry to the absurd theater was a natural one for Grass, as he reveals in a discussion held in Hamburg on October 19, 1961:

Up to now I have written poetry, plays and prose: all three disciplines are, with me, based on dialogue—even poetry. The transition from poetry to plays took place as follows: poetry was written in the form of dialogue and then expanded. That was shortly after the War. Then, slowly and gradually, stage directions were added; and then I developed my first play, in addition to my main profession at that time, that of a sculptor. Thus I wrote, in a comparatively short time from 1954 to 1957, four plays and two one-acters which contain, as do the poetry and the prose, fantastic and real elements, one revising and contradicting the other.[1]

The first play, assigned by Tank to the year 1954 and published in *Akzente*,[2] is a one-acter whose title, *Beritten hin und zurück* (Back and Forth, Mounted) points to the theme of arriving nowhere, and this characterizes the Theater of the Absurd. In its inconsequential way, it is concerned with literary theory and might well have been intended as a preliminary introduction to Grass' dramatic work, as it bears the subtitle "Ein Vorspiel auf dem Theater," a reference to the Prelude in the Theater which precedes the first part of Goethe's *Faust*. Just as in *Die Blechtrommel* the exemplary Wilhelm Meister lurks ironically behind Oskar's ignoble life story, so here the confidence of an earlier age contrasts with the uncertainty. Goethe's Prelude is a rhymed discussion between a Director, a Playwright and a "Comic Person" on the subject of the drama. As is proper to an orderly world, each of the three has his contribution to make to the discussion, which is opened and closed by the Director. In Grass' prelude we are at once plunged into a world plagued with doubt, one whose absurdities serve to demonstrate "the painful fact that there are no real answers." The Clown opens the proceedings, seated

[43]

on a rocking horse. As the other two, the Critic and the Playwright, seem to rely on the clown for any inspiration that may be available, the rocking horse must be regarded as a modern Pegasus.

The Clown immediately complains about the absence of categories; he is, he declares, no longer appreciated at the circus because ordinary people—his employers for instance—are more comic than he is. The Critic and the Playwright, together with the Actor who now joins them, have no solutions to offer, except to suggest replacing the wooden horse by a motorcycle (one of them has seen Cocteau's film *Orphée*). They waver uncertainly between comedy and tragedy while the Critic helplessly proposes a combination of the two plus a touch of surrealism (Beckett's theater is invoked at this point). For all their uncertainty, however, they insist that the Clown dismount from his childish rocking horse; equally determined to remain mounted, he tries to distract them with nonsense talk.

The Playwright has an inspiration and causes to appear on stage a bed in which, the Actor pretends, his wife is lying; but the Clown still refuses to dismount. The love interest which has been literally hauled on stage, refuses to develop, nor are matters helped even by reference to another film, Jean Louis Barrault's *Les Enfants du Paradis* with all its promising wealth of clowns, harlequins, whores, and picturesque situations. The Critic in desperation brings the Clown's daughter on stage, while the Clown feigns death, clinging to the neck of his rocking horse. Matters begin to look promising when it emerges that the daughter is engaged to a film-cutter, but that her father opposes the marriage.

Inspired by this fine conventional plot, the Critic eagerly quotes the Comedian's words from Goethe's "Vorspiel" "Greift nur hinein ins volle Menschenleben" (Plunge into life and give them human drama). The Clown, however, persists in his absurdities; he will have nothing to do with the cinema and pretends to find his future son-in-law's position as film-cutter incomprehensible: "What is that, a film-cutter? Either film or cutter, either cut or filmed!"

The film-cutter enters and reports that the Clown once enticed him into the circus ring only for the purpose of humiliating him in front of his employers. The Critic doubts the value of this comic episode (which involves sweaty socks), but the Playwright persists in believing in its tragic potentiality. The piece ends inconclusively with the Critic and the Playwright discussing episodes for a comedy which will end with inflation, mass unemployment, and war that destroys the world. In this plot the Clown is to be lynched by the mob; the Critic, however, who has the last word, doubts that he will arrive in time, in which case the result will be a comedy rather than a tragedy. They depart, leaving the Clown on his rocking horse.

The Clown-poet's persistence in his childish perspective was to be justified by *Die Blechtrommel* which successfully views the modern world from an infantile standpoint. The play's real theme, the impossibility of writing a play, is demonstrated, in the manner of Ludwig Tieck or Luigi Pirandello, by putting the theater on the stage. Conventional plots (for example, the love triangle) and symbols (for example, Death as a red-nosed comedian) are rejected or fail through lack of cooperation from the Clown who shows his continual awareness of the absurdity of the world by remaining on his rocking horse. The idea, amusing enough, fails to rescue the play from a certain sluggishness. The "Dramaturg," for example, is anxious to prevent the Clown from being monopolized by television companies but has no confidence in his (or anyone else's) theatrical instinct; nor is he at all sure how to regard the traditional categories of comedy and tragedy. The general situation, in which a director of the Theater of the Absurd is himself bewildered by its absurdities, is amusing, but it has not been dramatically developed. The play was not performed until 1959, in fact, after *Die Blechtrommel* had made Grass well known.

The first of Grass' dramas to be staged was *Hochwasser* (The Flood), written in 1955 and performed by the Frankfurt Student Theater in 1957. It was first printed in *Akzente,* and a slightly revised version was published by Suhrkamp in 1963.[3] While the setting is Noah's flood, the first scene revals Noah, an anxious householder in a respectably furnished ark, fussing over his collection of historical inkwells. His sister-in-law, Betty, is glancing through the family photo album while the daughter, Jutta, for lack of anything better to do, is conducting a listless affair with Henn—young, naïve, and hopelessly in love. The combination of ancient, archetypal catastrophe and modern scenery recalls Thornton Wilder's *The Skin of Our Teeth.*

The bourgeois calm is interrupted by the emergence—from a packing case which Noah believed to contain harmless domestic objects—of Noah's prodigal son Leo and his friend Kongo, an ex-boxer. They are cynical tramps and social outcasts who recall, in Brecht's words, "the great flood breaking over the bourgeois world." [4] Leo, offensive to everyone, and especially to Henn, is sent to join the rats sheltering on the roof, while Kongo skillfully occupies himself with a very willing Jutta. Grass adopted the suggestion, embodied in *Beritten hin und zurück,* and adorned his plot with a love triangle.

The rising waters force the others to join Henn on the roof; yet there is no real anxiety, for everyone seems aware that the emergency will end. The optimism of Betty, who has been sewing sunshades throughout the heavy rain and the moral laxness around her, proves fully justified when the floods recede, the rats prepare for a new era of prosperity (their appetites whetted by a delicious rainbow), Noah starts to order his collections, and Henn sulkily returns to Jutta. Leo and Kongo depart for more congenial climes, taking with them one of Noah's clocks. The final return of order is marked by the emergence from a grandfather clock of an official wearing an armband with a white dove design and anxious to obtain an exact assessment of damages.

The absurd parable is by no means impenetrable. Everyone except the intellectual Henn understands the rhythm of alternating catastrophe and normality. Kongo and Aunt Betty never interfere with each other's activities, and Jutta regrets, but is resigned to, the departure of her lover and a future with Henn. The course of the world has something of the senseless mechanical motion of the clock from which the inspector emerges at the end. Its pointless absurdity is underlined by the fact that the corrupt and brutal Leo and Kongo, in their capability and self-assurance, do not compare unfavorably with the tameness of the Noah household, just as Tulla in *Hundejahre* is refreshing in comparison with her subdued admirer Harry and the obliging Jenny. For this reason, catastrophe is not always unwelcome to everyone, especially to Jutta who says to Kongo: "As long as it rains, you'll stay with me. And if it rains again sometime, for a long, long time, then you'll come back." [5]

Comment on the action is provided by the rats Strich (Plain) and Perle (Purl). They notice, for example, that the flood is receding:

STRICH: I think we'd better be . . .
PERLE: You mean . . .
STRICH: Exactly. If I know them, they'll start to set traps and carry on as they always did.
PERLE: It really hasn't been too bad here. Tell me, if we stayed here, in style, as a sort of symbol that things are getting better . . . ?
STRICH: It wouldn't work with that lot, believe me, Perle. They'd misunderstand it. People nowadays have no feeling for genuine symbols. If we were doves now, true-blue doves of peace . . . [6]

The rats are fully aware that their kind traditionally leave sinking ships, but they realize, with sturdy common sense, that if they were to stay, the simple symbolism of their action would be inappropriate in an absurd world. After all, Wilhelm Emrich and other critics have declared that in modern literature the symbol has been replaced by the cipher, bare of traditional associations.[7] At the same time, their departure is a hint that the catastrophe is due to recur; it is a parallel to the sewing of sunshades at the height of the rains, an indication of the cyclical nature of human affairs.

A similarly disconcerting combination of realistic dialogue and grotesque events characterizes the next play, *Onkel, Onkel* (Mister, Mister), the first version of which was completed in 1956 and performed in Cologne in 1958.[8] A revised version was published in 1965. This play is longer (four acts, each with an introductory prelude) and more strictly absurd in that the autonomy and ambivalence of the object receives more attention that it does in *Hochwasser*. Objects, and especially his revolver, working in categories that have no relation to any recognized system of morality or immorality, prevent the murderer Bollin, a frustrated, systematic man, from proceeding coldbloodedly from one murder to another.

The childishly irrational element in the plot is apparent from the first prelude in which the girl Sprotte and the boy Jannemann are discovered discussing the murderer who is sleeping on a park bench. They adopt the knowing tones of social workers, or of the rats in *Hochwasser*: "I bet he doesn't have a mother and father" and "was an only child." They chant a song of a type encountered in all of Grass' early plays except *Beritten*, childish in content but earnest in context, the expression of a world where the structures and categories created by the intellect have no validity. The children are to repeat this song at the end of the play when they have shot the murderer with his own revolver:

> Onkel, Onkel haste ein Ding
> Onkel, nur ein kleines Ding,
> Irgend so ein Ding.[9]

("Uncle, uncle, don't you have a thing,/ Uncle, only a little thing,/ just a thing.")

His self-respect injured, Bollin hides under the bed of a sixteen-year-old girl, intent on rape and murder. When he emerges, however, the girl is not alarmed but warns him that she has influenza and invites him to help her with a crossword puzzle. He ends, comic paper fashion, by holding a skein of wool for her mother who reminds him to take his revolver with him when he departs: "You've left your thing there on the bedside table. Do you always carry it about?" [10] She classifies the revolver with other objects by recalling her late husband's habit of carrying a little toy car in his pocket.

The foiled murderer contents himself with stealing the doll Pinkie, on which he is seen practicing stabbing and shooting in the Prelude to Act Two. In this act, he plans to trap a forester and bury him alive (a similar plan has already succeeded). Attracted by Bollin's imitation of a cuckoo, the forester becomes trapped in a pit. He is rescued by the children Sprotte and Jannemann who ask him to explain some pine cones they have collected. In the course of the botany lesson, the forester and the children depart, leaving the frustrated murderer to fill in the pit.

The absurdity of the episode and its remoteness from logical categories is complete in that the forester does not consciously employ subterfuge to escape from the murderer. Trapped in the pit, he is not alarmed but, like an automaton, sustains his role as a pedagogue and a nature lover. When the children appear, he is displeased at the disturbance and gives vent to his annoyance in a schoolmasterly cliché: "These city-bred children! They grow up with houses all around them and go to the zoo perhaps once a year at the most." [11] He is so absorbed in this role that he never observes the danger that threatens him.

Bollin now seeks his victim in the world of grand opera, the soprano Mimi Landella. Her photographer fiancé is dumbly obedient like the rest, too preoccupied to be alarmed. For the sake of the excellent publicity, she is only too willing to allow Bollin to murder her photogenically in the bath. She overreaches herself, however, when she makes advances to Bollin in the hope of persuading him to become an opera singer. He departs hastily, crying "Bollin is normal." [12]

The prelude to the last act sees Bollin arranging to meet a victim, but the children trick him into giving up "the thing," after which they shoot him and depart, singing.

Although the conclusion is prefigured in the first act, the absence. of dramatic or dialectical development makes the total effect that of a one-acter expanded to fill a whole evening. Yet Marianne Kesting is surely mistaken in explaining the weakness of Grass' plays, including this one, by the absence of "sociological awareness." [13] The underlying idea is striking enough, the weakness lying in the dramatic execution. Bollin, the murderer, formerly successful in his chosen career, now, for no apparent reason, finds his aims frustrated.

The relationship of this situation to a broader reality is adumbrated in the Prelude to the second act wherein Bollin, stabbing and maltreating the doll, pretends to receive the congratulations of an imaginary superior officer: "Very good, Bollin, carry on!" [14] There are times when war and murder are not only accepted activities, but are also attended by success and aided by circumstance. Then suddenly and inexplicably, they cease to be so, with the result that the formerly successful practitioner finds himself frustrated at every turn, entangled by objects and events that no longer aid him. The absurdity lies in the fact that human beings have no rational control over this situation. The murderer, the gamekeeper, and the widow go on playing their assigned roles in a preoccupied fashion, while the real control over events lies elsewhere, in a region represented by the self-willed revolver.

This disconcerting fact is the subject of Grass' next play, *Noch zehn Minuten bis Buffalo* (Ten Minutes to Buffalo). Written in 1957, it was first performed in 1959 at Bochum and in Berlin's Schillertheater and has been a great favorite with German student theaters ever since. Wolfgang Hildesheimer has called this one-acter "a small token, so to speak, of the instability of the world." [15] The title, derived from Theodor Fontane's ballad, "John Maynard," is based on the well-known American folksong about the Lake Erie steersman who remains at his post when a fire breaks out aboard his steamer half an hour before it reaches Buffalo. At the sacrifice of his own life, he brings the vessel safely to Buffalo, and his coffin is followed by ten thousand weeping mourners.

The earnest, heroic striving and simple drama of Fontane's ballad is transposed into absurd pointlessness. The play opens with Krudewil and Pempelfort at the controls of a steam engine speeding toward Buffalo at ninety miles an hour, but, in reality, rusty and immobile in an Alpine meadow. Nearby, the painter Kotschenreuther is painting nautical scenes, explaining to the cowherd Axel that such outmoded distinctions as between "cow" and "ship," "professor" and "buttercup" must be eliminated. The two dilettante railwaymen carry on their own unreal drama, worrying about the coal supply, rejoicing at the approach of Buffalo and wrestling dramatically on a swaying tender. They have apparently served as seamen, so that much of their conversation has the nautical flavor appropriate to the title of the play. Surely enough, they meet "Frigate," their former captain, a sturdy woman in admiral's uniform smoking three cigars. At her behest, all three row off on foot across the meadows, while their cries of the "thar she blows" type die away into the distance. The last prop of reality is knocked away when the cowherd Axel, the only normal character, climbs into the derelict locomotive and shows not the slightest surprise when it steams off the stage.

The impossibility of communication in a world which cannot maintain simple distinctions among cows, ships, and locomotives becomes the central theme of Grass' next play, *Die bösen Köche* (The Wicked Cooks), his first to be performed in the United States. The plot concerns two warring groups of cooks in quest of the secret recipe for a mysterious, but desirable, repulsive soup which is gray and tastes of ashes. The holder of this secret is known as "the Count," although his baptismal name is Herbert Schymanski. The corps-de-ballet of cooks use threats, cunning, and persuasion, and finally offer the Count the nurse Martha as a wife if he promises to reveal his secret. But when the cooks demand fulfillment of his part of the bargain, the Count apologizes: "I am very sorry. . . . I have told you often enough that it is not so much a recipe as experience, living knowledge, constant change. You will probably be aware of the fact that no cook has ever succeeded in cooking the same soup twice." He adds by way of explanation: "The last few months, and life with Martha, have made this experience superfluous. I have forgotten it." [16] Since he has not kept his promise, however, the Count and his wife commit suicide.

This play, then, states that no statement can be made. In the Berlin premiere of 1962, produced by Walter Henn—to whose memory *Hundejahre* is dedicated—the Count wore a mask that suggested the face of Grass with its well-known moustache. This created an absurd circular structure by making the incommunicable recipe correspond to the meaning of the play. [17] The inadequacy of language is underlined by the choreographic element in which rival bands of cooks swarm across the stage, competing with, or being assisted by, soldiers with red armbands. The play opens with the chief cook blowing into a huge trumpet, out of which another cook emerges. Soon the whole stage is filled with white-clad figures chanting "The night is full of cooks." Extensive use is made of trapdoors, platforms, film, and a cacophonous musical score.

Beneath the infantile surface is a strain of mocking religiosity expressed through kneeling and liturgical chanting (the play opens on a Sunday). Indeed, Martin Esslin designates this play as an ambitious attempt to transmute a religious subject into poetic tragicomedy, pointing out an obvious analogy between the repulsive soup, around which the play circles, and the Eucharist.[18] This interpretation would be in keeping with the ascetic significance of repulsive brews of all kinds in Grass' works. The religious analogy is heightened by a scene in which Martha, the nurse, washes the Count's feet shortly before his death.

The play emphasizes its central ambiguity by hovering between tragedy and comedy, between the childish and earnest aspects of persecution, and also by means of such nonsense songs as "What could be sweeter than salt." The inherent senselessness of the whole is confirmed in the concluding scene when the cooks start to run away after the suicide of the Count and Martha. The cook's only explanation is: "It's because of my legs." Another cook, remaining behind to polish the tuba, comments: "There he goes. But I feel something happening in my legs, too." [19]

Thus the senseless movement of the beginning is resumed at the end, with nothing achieved, while the central theme dissolves into abstractions and mystery.[20] Futility and absurdity have been amply —too amply—demonstrated. Marianne Kesting justly criticizes Grass for having expanded the piece, by means of choreography and stage effects, into a five-act play.[21] The fact that Grass withdrew his next absurd play *Zweiunddreissig Zähne* (Thirty-two Teeth)[22] suggests that he had reached an impasse.

CHAPTER 4

Die Blechtrommel (The Tin Drum)

NOT until Grass came to write his novels was he really successful in employing the obsessive, sometimes highly individual images which objectify the world from which they spring. Broadly speaking, this world is the contemporary world seen, in the manner of the Theater of the Absurd, as an activity without meaning, purpose, or sane unifying principle. More specifically, this world is Langfuhr, the working-class suburb of the former city of Danzig, where Grass was born on October 16, 1927, some three years after Oskar, the narrator and hero of *Die Blechtrommel*. Childhood provided Grass with important motifs and themes: cruelty, superstition, indefinable fears, and an affinity for the repulsive. Above all, Grass' object-dominated world requires the child's vivid recollection of the world about him, coupled with an adult's precision in recording it. For all his grotesqueness, Oskar, the dwarf with an adult intelligence, corresponds to the actual truth of the author's perspective.

The child's perspective gives Grass' novels an undertone of an exile's nostalgia. The nostalgia, however, has an accidental character —the air of being a byproduct of the narrative—so that it is completely inoffensive and unsentimental. Above all, the child's perspective finds itself, by and large, in harmony with the evil and insanity of the surrounding world; and this harmony is a devastating commentary on the world. Spoken by Oskar Matzerath, the mad dwarf, the opening phrase of *Die Blechtrommel*, "Admittedly, I am the inmate of a nursing home," is an announcement of his fitness for the role of commentator.

Oskar's madness has no historic parallels and none of the associations with Nietzsche, Hölderlin, and Beethoven that lend grandeur to Thomas Mann's Adrian Leverkühn. Oskar is not a case of "O, what a noble mind is here o'erthrown," but rather of "a tale told by an idiot/ Full of sound and fury, signifying nothing."

Die Blechtrommel (The Tin Drum)

The sound and fury are represented, in the first place, by the title's tin drum which Oskar belabors to summon up the past. The drum is childish as well as militaristic and aggressive. Suitably enough, the original wielder of the drum was Hitler, whom General von Lossow contemptuously described as "the drummer" at the 1924 trial, an epithet which Hitler, in his final speech, turned into a compliment.[1] Brecht, in his poem "Beginn des Krieges" (Beginning of the War), also calls Hitler "der Trommler" (the drummer).[2]

In spite, or because, of his unusual circumstances, the narrator is anxious to prove his complete orthodoxy; and soon after he has introduced himself and his attendant, Bruno, he inserts a sententious paragraph implying that he intends to eschew the pretentious contrivances of modernism and write a straightforward, old-fashioned narrative:

One can start a story in the middle and proceed to spread confusion, boldly striding backwards and forwards. One can affect modernity, do away with time and distance and afterwards announce, or have it announced, that one has, at last and none too soon, solved the time-space problem. One can also assert, at the very beginning, that today it is impossible to write a novel, but then—behind one's own back, so to speak— write something really sensational and emerge as the very last of the novelists. (p. 11)

Actually, however, far from beginning at the beginning, Oskar begins his narrative in his West German present before embarking on his excursion through the past. Repeated reference is made to a friend named Klepp, for example, and to a lawyer who pays regular visits to Oskar in his ward. What is more, this pattern is repeated throughout the novel, with past and present placed in uneasy juxtaposition. This not only creates the characteristic atmosphere of doubt, but is, in its apparent absurdity, true to reality since a narrator's recollection of past events is mingled with the present.

The perspective, so elaborately described at the beginning of the novel, similarly combines the propagation of uncertainty with adherence to the truth. As noted in our introductory chapter, the attendant Bruno peers through the peephole while Oskar looks out; Oskar describes his position as being "in front of" the peephole, with Bruno relegated to standing "behind" it. From the material Oskar provides, Bruno makes grotesque figures of knotted string dipped in plaster-of-paris, although "whether he is an artist is a question best left aside" (p. 11). The wavering perspective, here as in *Hundejahre*, hints at the presence of the author behind his fictitious narrator. The lurking presence of the real narrator accounts for Oskar's frequent shifts from one side of the peephole to the other, so that personal confession is mingled with personal testimony, the cognizant subject being included in the object described.

Before Oskar commences his narrative, the question arises whether Bruno should color his string shapes. Oskar is forced to conclude that there is, after all, a demand for color; for his visitors do not like the unrelieved white of his ward and scratch the paint with scissors or draw indecent figures. Thus prompted, he orders virgin white paper (causing, Bruno reports, the salesgirl to blush) which he proceeds to soil with his chronicle. In this way the colors that recur throughout the work are introduced—the white of the ward and the nurses, the black of the Black Cook and the eels, the red of blood and fire. In the prevailing uncertainty it is, of course, impossible to assign to these colors a simple "symbolic" function, for they refuse to conform to tidy categories.[3] White signifies not only "purity" but also the confined monotony of Oskar's ward and the retrogression to childhood represented by the little white cot which he still occupies at the age of thirty. The colorful, active life of Oskar's grandfather is shot through with the red of flames. The red-and-white of Oskar's drum recalls both the Polish flag and the red, black, and white flag of Nazi Germany, and so on. After all, the wicked cooks of the play are white (as is the whale in *Moby Dick*),[4] while snow plays a part in the persecution of Jenny and Amsel in *Hundejahre*.

Monotone grays and browns predominate when Oskar opens his chronicle in the year 1899, with his grandmother burning potato plants in the endless plains of the Vistula in what was then West Prussia. Using long obsolete German place names, he designates the exact place where she sat, preferring precision to nostalgia:

[She sat] near Bissau, still nearer the brickworks, before Ramkau, behind Viereck, in the direction of the road to Brenntau, between Dirschau and Karthaus, with her back to the forest of the Goldkrug. . . . (pp. 11–12)

While she is sitting by the fire, Joseph Koljaiczek enters the scene, pursued across the muddy fields by two gendarmes; the sober tale takes a sudden turn to the grotesque when Joseph dives under the grandmother's skirts for refuge. It is presumably while the grandmother, Anna, is being questioned by the suspicious policeman,

[54]

Oskar's mother is conceived, although Anna, for the sake of propriety, denies this.

Still dwelling on "The Wide Skirt" which provides the chapter's heading, Oskar describes his grandmother's habit of wearing four skirts, one over the other, and how, on Saturday, the dirtiest of the current four was replaced by a clean one in orderly peasant routine. In this fashion the wide skirt comes to reveal its central function in this part of Oskar's narrative, that of a cipher of the world before 1914, "the golden age of security," as Stefan Zweig has called it.[5] Grass enlivens this cliché by embodying it in an objective correlative that covers many aspects of this famed security, including the sexual, without neglecting the steady regularity persisting in the turbulence. The refuge of Anna Bronski's wide skirts is freely offered to Koljaiczek and often sought by Oskar in later times. It is a characteristic of Grass' methods that the narrator (Oskar, in this case) is unaware of the significance of skirt and drum.

The drum is first mentioned in the second chapter. Oskar, who has permission to play it for a few hours every day, consults it as an oracle that conjures up the past. We learn of further adventures of Anna Bronski and Koljaiczek after their hasty marriage. Wanted by the police for setting fire to German sawmills as a gesture of Polish patriotism (red flames and whitewashed walls), Joseph takes up work as a log rafter under an assumed name. A journey to Kiev gives Grass an opportunity to present a panorama of pre-1914 Eastern Europe as the steamer makes its way from Germany to Russia along the Vistula, Bug, Pripet, and Dnieper. He dwells on the military history of the region, "created for cavalry attacks, for a division of Uhlans wheeling left in the sandbox" (p. 28). The theme of war introduces, with characteristic planned casualness, the clash between Pole and German which occurs when the foreman of the rafters, a Prussian named Dückerhoff, recognizes Joseph. The encounter of Pole and German is yet another recurring theme in Grass' novels (both Mahlke in *Katz und Maus* and Matern in *Hundejahre* struggle, half-consciously, to reconcile these warring elements in themselves), and Grass now takes the opportunity, through his narrator, to renounce any clichés in his depiction of this struggle. Between Dückerhoff and Koljaiczek there were "no political quarrels, German-Polish knifings, nor was there the attractive background of a good, solid mutiny on board, arising from social abuses." The story also dispenses with sentimental reconciliations. Instead, German-

Polish relations take their normal course in this little incident. His business in Kiev completed, Dückerhoff returns to Danzig. His route is exactly traced, and the reader observes that he passes through territory that the course of history will subsequently transfer from Germany to Poland.

Dückerhoff reports his suspicions to the police, as befits a good citizen, and is never heard from again. As a result, Joseph's log-raft is shadowed from the time it crosses into Germany. On its arrival at Danzig, a police launch sets out to make the arrest. Throwing off his lethargy, Joseph flees across the rafts, jumps into the water and is presumably drowned just as a Prince of the Imperial Household is launching the "Columbia," a luxury liner for the American service. Realizing the Polish capacity for surviving against heavy odds, Oskar advances a theory that he escaped to the United States. In this incident, Grass, without contrition or condemnation, mirrors German-Polish relations in all their vicious inconclusiveness. The chapter ends as the fire-raiser Koljaiczek, hunted by a powerful police apparatus, is submerged by the launching of the mighty German ship. Yet, while according to vague rumor the irrepressible Pole is resurrected in America as a prosperous businessman, the "Columbia," we are informed in the next chapter, is lost in the First World War.

With the same deliberate absence of explanation and protest, the author tacitly compares the hospital ward of the cramped, neurotic West German present with an earthy but colorful and wide-ranging past summed up in the "Wide Skirt" of the chapter's heading. The third chapter follows the already familiar pattern, with a grotesque and puzzling title ("Moth and Light-bulb") and an excursion into the narrator's West German present. In his hospital ward, Oskar tries, without much success, to find an understanding audience for his grandmother's adventures, but his West German friends receive the story with incomprehension and indifference or as material for parody. The celebrated dividing line between past and present—the year 1914—has made the story alien to them, and when his friends have departed, Oskar resumes his narrative and tacitly acknowledges the change by beating his drum "in that quicker, jerkier rhythm that all had to obey from August 1914 onwards" (p. 41). Elements of this new rhythm are hinted at in the fact that Klepp, one of Oskar's visitors, is a jazz enthusiast and confirmed Marxist.

Oskar's narrative moves swiftly to the armistice, when "peace treaties, giving rise to other wars, were patched up." For example, the Danzig Free State was formed and placed under the League of

Nations, and Oskar traces with lunatic precision the course taken
by the strange boundaries of the new territory as it cuts through the
familiar landscape in which his grandmother had been seated. The
public event is ironically reflected in Oskar's petit-bourgeois world
when Oskar's mother marries a German, Alfred Matzerath, while,
as it later turns out, retaining a passionate relationship with her
Polish cousin, Jan Bronski. All of Grass' novels present this characteristic pattern of official history alternating with obscure, often
scurrilous or fantastic biography and low-life fiction, somewhat in
the manner of Döblin's novel *Berlin—Alexanderplatz* (1929).

The parallel between public and private events is especially
striking here, for if Matzerath comes originally from the Rhineland,
Bronski is not, strictly speaking, a Pole but of the same Slav race
as Oskar's grandparents. He is, in fact, one of the Cassubians
(*Kaschuben*) characterized in Theodor Fontane's novel *Effi Briest* as
a fine-looking but—from the Prussian point of view—unreliable
people. Jan Bronski adopts Polish nationality in 1920—possibly out
of pique at being jilted by Oskar's mother—and obtains a position
in the Polish Post Office in Danzig. The contrast between Bronski
and Matzerath is partly that between the introvert and the extrovert,
the former being quiet, sly, and passionate while the latter is jovial,
loud, and rather foolish (but an excellent cook). With the master-
fulness that is typical of Grass' women, Agnes Bronski takes as a
husband the one who cooks while she works in the grocer's shop she
has inherited; she takes the other as a lover. This arrangement provides a derisory parallel to the arrangement made concerning Danzig
on the international level.

The parallel must not be taken too far, however. The grocer's shop
flourishes under the competent guidance of Oskar's mother. It and
the adjoining apartment are described with the vivid freshness of
a child first growing aware of the outside world. But the fresh eye
is coupled with an adult's awareness, for Oskar points out the specifically lower-middle-class nature of his surroundings. It is against
this appropriate background that the historical events are seen. The
account of Oskar's birth, which concludes the chapter, "explains" in
grotesque fashion the novelist's gift for combining adult perspicacity
with infantile naïveté: "I was one of those infants, sharp of hearing,
whose spiritual development is complete at birth, and from then on
needs only to be confirmed." So acute was Oskar's intelligence that
he can recall his birth, which ran smoothly, as he comments with
lofty detachment, "apart from the obligatory rupture of the peri-

neum" (p. 49). This miraculous birth, which scorns the slow educational process of the "Entwicklungsroman," recalls that of Rabelais' Gargantua who, when he was born, yelled loudly and clearly "à boyre, à boyre."

Oskar especially recalls a moth that drummed against a light bulb (60 watts, manufactured by Osram) during his birth. The incident, recalled in minute detail, causes the narrative to linger over a characteristic word play on drums and drummers. With this sound of drumming, and with the moth and the light, Oskar's birth in 1924 takes place under threatening omens. It is to be noted, however, that Oskar's world is a chaos where reality has been denuded of its symbolic value. The moth, the conventional symbol of a creature threatened, is here the source of threatening drumfire. It is impossible to distinguish between victim and persecutor, between innocence and guilt. Oskar, too, is bewildered, but inwardly resolves to follow his mother's suggestion, which he overhears, and to acquire a tin drum.

In an abrupt switch to the narrator's present, Oskar's next point of departure is a photo album rescued from Danzig and containing pictures extending from the turn of the century to Oskar's postwar life in Düsseldorf. The album links the sections of this rambling novel and also serves as a peg on which to hang a lightly camouflaged discussion of the novelist's method—a matter which occupies Oskar's attention more than he is prepared to admit. He begins by observing how "the photographic art of the fin de siècle has degenerated into the utilitarian photograph of today." Where Joseph Koljaiczek faces the camera, broad and confident in his fireman's uniform, the best that Oskar and Klepp can do with their mass-produced passport photographs is to cut them up and reassemble them as grotesque mosaics. This apparently foolish prattle is, in effect, a discussion of the modern novelist's method. Why does he use a "montage" of realistic details instead of presenting a straightforward portrait? The answer is, of course, that "montage" is a means of coming to grips with reality in a more uniform society. Oskar adduces the sadness felt by Klepp and himself as an example. This sadness is "ungegenständlich," i.e., objectless, without obvious cause—the word is repeated three times—and cannot be captured by any other method.

Oskar and his creator do not allow this discussion of artistic. methods—discreetly disguised as pointless chatter—to distract them from the main plot, for by means of the photo album the story of the engagement and marriage of Oskar's mother is rapidly summarized in the manner of the cinema, which Oskar loves to attend and which he is presumably parodying at this point. The triangular relationship between Oskar's mother and her two lovers is the subject of some ambiguous geometrical terminology.

Oskar invites the reader, if he wishes, to find "cosmic significance" (p. 61) in the triangle by relating it to the world outside, i.e., to the German-Polish quarrel over Danzig after 1919. At any rate, Oskar, with his discerning dwarf's eye, does not hesitate to find the whole commonplace story, with its Central European and petit-bourgeois background "significant for the future." This ironic passage is one of the few direct hints at an association between Oskar's microcosm and the macrocosm of public events. In fact, the nature of this association is unforced and its discovery left to the reader, so that Oskar's reputation as a teller of simple tales is left untarnished. Yet the association is both general—it was in Oskar's lower-middle-class circles that the Nazi movement had its most massive support—and particular. Thus Oskar does not forget to state that his parents' wedding took place at the time of the Treaty of Rapallo, a pact of economic and military aid between Germany and the new state of Soviet Russia signed in 1922. The adultery which Oskar's mother committed, we are told, on her very wedding day creates a humorous parallel, if one cares to draw it, to the shaky, opportunistic nature of this and subsequent Soviet-German treaties.

A later photograph also hints at a threat lurking under the harmless, commonplace exterior. It shows Oskar and his parents in front of a plank fence. His mother is wearing a Russian blouse of a type popular in the 1920's, so that the scene recalls the Czar's family, later murdered by the revolutionaries. Finally, there is a photograph of Oskar on his third birthday. He explains that he deliberately ceased to grow at this age, rejecting thereby the mundane possibility of inheriting his father's shop in favor of a greatness which he describes as "Messianic." Oskar's infantility, coupled with an adult self-destructive will and the urge for an illusory absolute power, plainly makes him a spokesman for his era.

Oskar's mysterious hint that "he remained a three-year-old" is expanded in the following chapter, whose title is taken from a non-sense rhyme. The reader learns that Oskar contrived an accident on his third birthday, a fall down the cellar steps that provided the world with an acceptable reason for his stunted physical development. With amusement Oskar notes that, by general consent, the blame is placed on Matzerath, the German. After four weeks in the hospital, Oskar's destructive powers come to their first fresh fruition. Marching about Danzig as a harbinger of the coming war, he shatters glass with his shrill, vibrating voice, "a chaste and therefore pitiless diamond" (p. 71).

By now Oskar has emerged as an "embodied expression" of the infantile destructive principle. The resemblance to the Expressionists extends to concrete details. Richard Sorge's early drama *Der Bettler* (The Beggar) thus includes an insane character who beats on a toy drum and entertains Messianic ambitions. The hero of Frank Wedekind's *Karl Hetman, der Zwergriese* (Karl Hetman, the Dwarf-Giant) is a crippled writer who is committed to a sanatorium and offered employment as a circus clown. Even Grass' word "zersingen," used to express Oskar's powers of shattering glass by singing, recalls not only Expressionist frenzy in general, but, more particularly, Benn's coinage "zergellend." [6]

While Oskar revels in his newly discovered powers, his mother is kept busy rejecting claims for broken windows. Oskar's destructive voice is not only very real, but it calls forth significant reactions from his environment. The company assembled at the Matzeraths is at first alarmed when Oskar's voice shatters a clock's glass, for the clock represents the world of order. On the other hand, the point is soon reached where Oskar's misdeeds are not always unwelcome to the grownup world, for when he shatters the light bulbs at his fourth birthday party, the company seizes the opportunity to pair off in a short but unappetizing orgy. A final paragraph, this time in the third person, records the inevitable deterioration. Later in his career, Oskar reports, he will use his peculiar talents out of an idle joy in destructiveness—a parodistic parallel to the career of any tyrant or revolutionary movement.

Before Oskar continues his autobiography with an account of his one-day school career, he occupies himself with the postwar world and the habits of his friend Klepp who works many hours in the composition of a time-table for his daily routine. Although Klepp is a member of the Communist Party, illegal in Western Germany, his chart is a comfortable affair that allows little time for agitation and propaganda activity. In postwar Germany, after the catastrophe, even revolutionaries respect time-tables and a regular routine. Oskar's account of his early youth implies the presence of an entirely different, harsher spirit in the early 1930's when the catastrophe was approaching. Even in Oskar's kindergarten a boy attacks Stephan, the son of Jan Bronski, on the grounds that he is "a dirty Pole," eliciting but a mild reproach from the elderly lady in charge of the children. The scene takes place near the Gutenberg memorial, an object which presides over another act of childish persecution in *Hundejahre.*

Oskar's mother is anxious that her son, in spite of his abnormality, enter the local Pestalozzi school. Oskar, however, with his anarchistic spirit, is resentful of his teacher and utters a shout that pulverizes her spectacles. Before he leaves the schoolyard with his mother for the last time, he is photographed standing in front of a blackboard on which is chalked "My first day at school."

By normal standards, the whole situation is full of pathos, but Oskar can see only fear, especially in the sentence on the board written in the "evil" script invented by Sütterlin (the "German" script taught in German schools until the 1940's). Fascinated, as earlier noted, by its hangman's nooses and jagged points, Oskar feels the urge to read, a skill he learns from a thick volume on Rasputin and his mistresses, although in every fourth lesson he asks for Goethe, Rasputin's complement. This compromise serves to define Grass' own approach which similarly mingles anarchistic imagination and disciplined art. When Oskar's area of perception extends to the complex of tenements in the working-class suburb of Langfuhr, the combination of childhood vividness and adult detachment with which he describes this proletarian landscape is, likewise, a reflection of the author himself. The overriding impression is, however, one of fear. Two features of the wider surroundings which Oskar begins to observe in this stage of his development embody this fear: the racks for carpet-beating, situated in every courtyard, and a soup made of urine, brickdust, and frogs prepared by a gang of children who compel Oskar to eat it.

The pessimism that inevitably accompanies experience causes Oskar to turn destructive; he becomes "a yeller without cause or reason." In a mood of despair after the bitter lesson of the repulsive soup, he climbs to the top of the Stockturm, a Brick Gothic tower that was one of the few medieval structures in Danzig to survive the war. From this point Oskar utters a shout that shatters the windows of the nearby State Theater—a parody of an Old Testament prophet uttering a curse over the doomed city. In the same vein of prophecy the Jewish toydealer, Markus, advises Oskar's mother to leave Bronski because he sees a time approaching when the German cause will prosper at the expense of the Polish. Actually, she will take Markus' advice by dying.

In an abrupt shift to the present, Oskar reflects that the scene of all these activities now lies in Poland and that Markus' prophecy was valid only for a short term. Germans today search for Poland "half with Chopin, half with revenge in their hearts" (p. 126). Their attitude is complex since it is determined by trading loans, regret for the past, and the resentment of refugees driven from their homes. They make the mistake of searching for Poland "with the soul," an ironical echo of Goethe's Iphigenia who longs for the land of the Greeks:

> Und an dem Ufer steh ich lange Tage,
> Das Land der Griechen mit der Seele suchend.

Realizing that the soul is irrelevant, Oskar emerges with an admiration for Poland's powers of survival, although it is continually divided among conquerors.

The next chapter, "The Tribune," continues the Goethe parody. In accordance with the convention of Goethe's *Wilhelm Meisters Theatralische Sendung* (Wilhem Meister's Theatrical Mission), the theater plays an important part in a young man's education. In Oskar's world, of course, conventions can exist only as their own parody. Thus his first contact with the stage is, farcically, the occasion when he breaks the windows of the State Theater. This leads to the desire for further contact, which duly takes place on Oskar's level: a visit to *Tom Thumb* and, in the summer of 1933, an open-air performance of Wagner's *The Flying Dutchman* which Oskar abruptly terminates.

This education receives a fitting climax in a circus visit, when Oskar first encounters the ageless, Goebbels-like midget Bebra who, recognizing Oskar's genius, advises him to turn to politics so that he can gain power in the coming age when "they will build tribunes, people the tribunes and preach our downfall from tribunes" (p. 134). Oskar's theatrical education has led him, by way of German folklore and Wagner, to the Nazi Party.

Oskar's "putative father," Matzerath, joins the Party in 1934 and proves to be a conscientious member. With increasing earnestness he advises Bronski to give up his position in the Polish Post Office. He also places Hitler's portrait in the place of honor above the piano from where it glares across at a displaced Beethoven on the opposite wall. In Thomas Mann's *Doktor Faustus* Beethoven is seen as the spiritual ancestor of Adrian Leverkühn whose music represents the coming era of technically accomplished barbarism. In *Die Blech-trommel*, the continuity of German history is farcically suggested by the simultaneous presence of Hitler and Beethoven in a lower-middle-class parlor.

Following Bebra's advice, and recognizing a congenial spirit in the brilliant hunchback Nazi agitator Löbsack, Oskar tries to take his rightful place on the speaker's platform at Party demonstrations. It is only when the Nazis refuse to see in him anything but the three-year-old boy whom he outwardly resembles that Oskar turns against the Party by hiding under the platform and beating out a waltz that cuts through the trumpets of the Hitler Youth and sets the spectators dancing. The mood rises to a frenzy when he strikes up a Charleston, whereupon Löbsack, making the best of a bad jab, joins in the dancing. Chance and circumstance have made Oskar into a resistance hero. His irrational powers have defeated those of Löbsack and the Nazis, and he can slip away in triumph to a heavy North German Sunday dinner.

Oskar can offer effective resistance to the Nazis because he taps the same sources of irrational power. Thus it is that, on the strength of his activities under the speakers' tribune, he lays no claim to any special virtue, certainly not to having been a member of the underground resistance. He is especially sardonic at the expense of those who remained in Germany during this era but who afterwards claimed to have offered inner, spiritual resistance to the regime ("interior emigration"). Oskar was no such "resistance hero." He disturbed meetings of all kinds—Communists, Catholic, Young Polish, and Vegetarian, and his powers cut across all man-made boundaries. "My work was destructive" he admits, explaining that during this period he also used his powerful voice to break shop windows and thus tempted innocent passersby to commit petty thefts.

The reactions are as varied as Oskar's victims: some succumb to the temptation, some hasten away, while others fall but afterwards give themselves up to the police. Oskar finds them all equally amusing and relishes the ridiculous moral perplexities he has caused, noting with glee the ineffectiveness of conventional systems of morality and liberal enlightenment. Even Oskar's irrationalism is not allowed the last word, however. The climax of Oskar's grotesque shoplifting is reached on a cold night in 1937 when he succeeds in tempting Jan Bronski into stealing a ruby necklace. The whole incident is adorned with onomatopoeia, suggestive of shattering glass, and with references to Parzival seeing drops of blood in the snow. Yet the elaborately presented episode, like so many other events of this period, fades out shortly after the war when the jewelry is exchanged for Lucky Strike cigarettes, the black market currency of a defeated Germany.

The customary return to the narrator's West German present in the next chapter, "Kein Wunder" (which means both "No Miracle" and "No Wonder"), shows him deprived of his miraculous voice. This impotence dates from the postwar period in Düsseldorf; but when Oskar resumes his chronicle, the reader can perceive its beginnings in the prewar past when his voice failed to shatter the stained-glass windows of the Church of the Sacred Heart. Needless to say, it is not virtue and enlightenment that defeat Oskar's infantile dynamic, but a related, rival magic. Frau Matzerath's church-going, on which Oskar accompanies her, is part of a regular round that includes her weekly visits to her lover, Jan Bronski. The interior of the church exercises on Oskar "the fascination of a red-haired woman." The bewitching powers of this "scarlet woman" are demonstrated by means of fragments from missals and prayers, a play with echoing phrases concerning "blood," "virgin," and "cross" uttered half in parody, half in admiration. Above all, a statue of the infant Jesus elicits irreverence and admiration from Oskar. He slings his drum around the neck of the statue; but the hoped-for miracle does not occur and Jesus does not beat the drum.

The preceding chapter has introduced a strain of religious parody, and this is carried across into the next chapter, "Good Friday Fare," which includes the notorious eel-catcher scene. Oskar's mother and father, inevitably accompanied by Jan Bronski, and Oskar himself go on a Good Friday outing to the seaside near Danzig. There they encounter a longshoreman fishing for eels and using a horse's head as bait. The sight of the eels squirming out of the head causes Oskar's mother to vomit; it also induces in her such a perverted taste for fish as to cause her death after an interval of some weeks during which she consumes great quantities with silent hysteria. In this manner she is expressing, Oskar believes, her disgust with the triangular relationship she had sustained for years, ultimately, perhaps, her disgust with life itself which takes such monstrous forms.

The incident possibly reflects the Good Friday scene in which Parzival, after an encounter with an elderly hermit, feels the urge to make his peace with God. Certainly, Oskar is convinced, his mother wished to leave Jan unencumbered in his career and that her disgust is directed against Matzerath, her official husband—a man whose inborn urge to yell, laugh, and applaud with the crowd made him, the reader is told, an early member of the Nazi Party. Yet, as usual, Grass guards against facile interpretation. Matzerath proves himself a considerate husband during his wife's lingering illness and is prepared to adopt the unborn child which, as he realizes, is probably not his own. At the funeral he behaves with appealing Protestant awkwardness, while Frau Matzerath's mother prays volubly in Cassubian, finally flinging herself on the coffin, loudly blaming Matzerath.

Before the first book ends on the verge of the Second World War, a number of grotesque incidents occur with Herbert Truczinski as their focus. Whereas the preceding chapters concern religion, these chapters concern, roughly speaking, history and politics. When Oskar first encounters Herbert, the latter is working as a waiter in a seaman's tavern. In his broad Danzig dialect, interspersed with fragments of Polish and English, he attempts to control his unruly clientele, a microcosm of Europe, who are always quarreling. The result is that Herbert is brought home in an ambulance once or twice every month. His back patterned with scars from frequent knifings, Herbert emerges from Oskar's account as a long-suffering member of the working classes whose injuries, his mother acutely suspects, are caused by his defense of such matters as the Republican cause in the Spanish Civil War.

Herbert is remarkable not only for the disinterestedness of his actions but for the workings of an active conscience. He is distressed when a sea captain dies of heart failure during a tavern brawl and at having to steal food during a period of unemployment. Herbert is not one of Grass' successful figures; he is strangely lifeless and comes dangerously close to contradicting the ambiguity of Grass' world by being merely symbolical, although Grass tries to avoid this by injections of grotesqueness and by hints at more complicated fields of reference. Thus the tavern proprietor is named Starbusch, plainly a reminiscence of Starbuck in *Moby Dick.*

Herbert's death is described in the chapter "Niobe." After weeks of listless unemployment, he obtains an apparently safe post as an attendant at the Danzig museum of local history. This museum, however, contains a menacing object, a figurehead from a Dutch vessel captured by two fifteenth-century Danzig seafarers. It has the form of a generously proportioned girl, painted green and known in the local dialect as "De griehne Marjell," although her official name is Niobe—the queen whose fourteen children were killed before her eyes. The Flemish girl who served as a model was burned as a witch, with the result that there is a curse attached to the figure. Many bloody events in Danzig history have been strangely associated with this figurehead and, in more recent times, it has brought about the deaths of various museum officials and visitors.

In his account, Oskar links its baleful influence with the destruction of Danzig at the end of the Second World War and attributes the comparative immunity of the other ancient Baltic seaport of Lübeck (now in Western Germany) to the wise refusal of its authorities to receive the figurehead into the museum. In fact, to some extent the figurehead resembles the town of Kaisersaschern in *Doktor Faustus*, which spreads its baleful influence, rooted in witchcraft, torture and superstition, to the present. While there is in Mann's Kaisersaschern an element of moral judgment—a condemnation of the direction taken by German history—Grass' figurehead operates in an amoral, senseless world. The irrational powers embodied in Niobe are expressed in an obscene episode. On the first day Herbert goes on duty without the protection of Oskar's superior magic, he commits suicide, clutching the figurehead in a grotesque embrace—a symbol of enlightenment and decency overcome by, and helpless before, the force of historical events.

In an abrupt turn to the present, Bruno enters Oskar's ward in Western Germany to remove the drum from his reach because he is disturbing the other patients with the noise. Bruno's action implies a prim apology for the violence of Herbert's death and serves, at the same time, as a reminder of the central part played by the drum as the object that calls the world's tune.

In spite of Oskar's promise to play softly in future and to have more regard for the other patients (namely, the readers), his drum, heedless of human wishes, is louder than ever in the next chapter, "Faith, Hope and Charity," which closes the First Book. The irrational, primitive violence that has been observed in obscure, private lives now enters the field of official history. It reaches a crescendo on the eve of the Second World War with the "Kristallnacht" of November 9, 1938, when members of the SA (the "Brownshirts"), on Goebbel's orders, raided synagogues and Jewish shops. In the Danzig pogrom, the toydealer Markus is found dead by the local Brownshirt bullies who wreck his shop. The raid on the toyshop is presented so as to emphasize the infantile destructive urge that here finds expression. The raiders slash open dolls and befoul the shop with excrement in the manner of overgrown children. As they have usurped Oskar's infantile role, he feels free to make amused adult comments, and notes the futility of writing "Jew swine" on the window before breaking it.

In their brown uniforms, Oskar tells us, the SA men all looked like the trumpet player Meyn. Yet when the narrative turns more fully to inspect this epitome of Brownshirt brutality, the result is puzzling and full of inconsistencies. Meyn had been a friend of Herbert Truczinski when they were both members of a Young Communist group. He appears at Herbert's funeral in uniform. On seeing him, Schugger Leo, a harmless eccentric who frequents the cemetery, flees in terror across the graves. Meyn is neither puzzled nor amused by Leo's behavior. On the contrary, he is perceptive enough to return home downcast at this "token of future misfortune." Overcome by melancholy and unaccustomed sobriety, Meyn beats the tomcats that are his sole companions and leaves them for dead. A neighbor, who has witnessed this, reports Meyn, and comically enough, he is expelled from the Brownshirts in spite of his attempts to make good through a display of destructive zeal during the raids on Jewish shops.

The episode serves as another illustration of Grass' implicit thesis that men have only limited control over their actions. Meyn's realization that his present course will lead to no good end finds incoherent expression in the incident of the cats. Yet his remorse serves no good or useful purpose; rather it aligns itself with the malevolent spirit that rules human affairs and, through Meyn, contributes its small quota to the current atrocities. Even the Christ Child of the approaching Advent season turns into the "heavenly gasman" whose spirit fills the world.

The malevolent rule extends from small affairs to big, as is indicated by the fact that one of Meyn's cats, killed on the eve of the war, is named "Bismarck," a comic parallel to the dismissal of the "Reichskanzler" by Kaiser Wilhelm II, which is often held to have led to a deterioration in the conduct of German policy and thus to the First World War. The approach of the Second World War is heralded by a tattoo of drumbeats, conveyed by means of a series of sentences beginning with the traditional fairy-tale opening, "Es war einmal" (Once upon a time), an indication of the infantile nature of what is to follow.

The Second World War

As the Second Book is to cover the Second World War, the title of the first section, "Schrott" (Scrap Metal), seems appropriate, for war is an insatiable consumer and creator of scrap metal. However, there are further implications. The scrap metal under discussion is being collected in Oskar's West German present, for, as the chapter opens, it is visitors' day at the sanatorium, and Maria, whom the attentive reader will remember as the young sister of Herbert Truczinzki, arrives with a new drum. The old drum, battered after the exertions of Book One, is solemnly handed over into her keeping to join the other drums which, at Oskar's lunatic insistence, she has been storing in her cellar. As she has done this since 1949, the year of the foundation of the modern *Bundesrepublik*, the reader can assume that a mocking reference is being made to the rearmament policy of Germany's new government, especially as Maria complains that the drums in her cellar are interfering with the storage of her winter potatoes (a sensible purpose for her cellar). Oskar's anxieties about the supply of drums derives from memories of the brief and terrible "drumless time" following the destruction of Markus' toyshop in 1938. The deprivation leads to an illness from which Oskar does not recover until he acquires a new drum after the German invasion of Poland in 1939. The drumless period is summarized as one of asceticism, a virtue which Grass recommends in his poetry as an antidote to the times.

But 1939 is no period for prolonged, ascetic abstention from the heady excitement that is embodied in Oskar's drum. The German invasion of Poland represents a resumption of the spirit of the "Kristallnacht." It finds a convenient equivalent, at Oskar's local level, in the attack (which did take place as a matter of historical fact) on the Post Office maintained by the Polish government in the Free State of Danzig. It is now the plain duty of Jan Bronski, a loyal Pole and postal official, to take part in the defense of this building, as the Warsaw authorities have ordered. The adult aspect of Oskar can understand Jan's reluctance to comply: "My putative father had such an exact and, for all his tenderly voluptuous fancies, realistic conception of war, that it was difficult, if not impossible, for him to be brave out of a sheer lack of imagination" (p. 279).

Oskar's infantile nature, however, prevails, ruled, as it is, by the all-powerful drum. His overriding urge is to visit the Post Office where the janitor, Kobyella—a veteran of Pilsudski's successful resistance to the Russian invasion of 1920—can repair his drum. It is at this point that the drum is specifically associated with the war. On the last day of August, 1939, the day before Hitler invaded Poland, Oskar contrives to meet Jan and lead him through the familiar streets, exactly designated, to the Post Office which is about to be attacked by the local German forces. To Jan's dismay, the German sentries do not prevent him, a well-dressed man, accompanied by a (apparently) three-year-old boy, from entering the besieged building.

If the permanently three-year-old Oskar represents the spirit of war, the German-Polish struggle is more specifically epitomized at this point by the letters, some bearing German, some Polish names of towns on the fluid borderline between the two peoples. The letters are stored in baskets that are soon to serve as beds for the wounded, but which at first serve as a bed for Oskar: "I slept in a washing-basket full of letters that wanted to go to Lodz, Lublin, Lwow, Torun, Krakow, and Czestochowa, which came from Lodz, Lublin, Lemberg, Thorn, Krakau, and Tschenstochau" (p. 268).

The skirmish itself is presented dialectically under two contrasting aspects. Before and after the main action, Polish martial glory is celebrated—the brave heart of Pilsudski, or the cavalry fighting against tanks. With a mixture of admiration and mockery, Pan Kiehot (Don Quixote) is invoked as "a pure-bred Pole of noble countenance." This romantic, patriotic aspect of the struggle against the German invaders is confronted by the aspect that brutal reality insists on, for in reality the romantic, melancholy Pole (Jan Bronski) is timid, while the brave man (Kobyella) is also callous. When the Post Office comes under fire, the terrified Jan exposes his leg in an absurd attempt to acquire a harmless wound, whereupon the Pilsudski veteran brutally assaults him. Before Kobyella can effect an effective kick with his lame foot, however, he is struck by a bullet and bedded down in a letter-basket in a dark room that serves as an emergency hospital. Here Jan finds refuge from the battle raging outside, while he passes the time playing *Skat* with the dying Kobyella and Oskar who drops the pretense of being a three-year-old. The game comes to an end only when the Germans burst in with their well-known cries of "Raus." The game of *Skat*, the jargon of which Grass cannot refrain from quoting, provides Jan with the necessary distraction. Absorbed in the game and still clutching a card, Jan faces arrest and execution with a calm indifference that amounts to bravery.

The incident of the Polish Post Office brings a new lease of life to Oskar who acquires a new drum from the nursery of the vacated apartment of the Postmaster. After the Post Office has been captured by the Germans, he points to Jan as one "who had dragged an innocent child into the Polish Post Office, to use it, in an inhuman Polish way, for stopping bullets" (p. 300). His cynicism knows no limits. When the authorities send Jan's mother a brusque letter which announces that her son has been executed but fails to state where, Oskar's explanation is: "They were considerate to the dependents, wanted to save them the expense of tending a far too expensive and flower-consuming mass grave" (p. 304). In this context, with the spirit of war triumphant, Hitler makes a brief appearance in Danzig. He has conquered Poland in eighteen days. His insignificance, as he is borne past at the tail end of a long adjectival phrase, corresponds to the implicit view of history that sees human beings as mere pawns at the mercy of more powerful forces. The narrator is, in any case, concerned with his own rather than with public affairs.

War does not enjoy so easy a victory as Oskar would have the reader imagine. Proud as he is of his cynical betrayal of Jan, he cannot deny that he had to spend some time in a hospital immediately after the ordeal in the Post Office. Moreover, the eccentric Schugger Leo compels Oskar to visit the distant cemetery where Jan was executed. It is true that Oskar recovers, but he receives another setback when, at Christmas, 1939, Matzerath fails to present him with a new drum to replace the one obtained from the Post Office.

The situation is rescued with the arrival of Maria as Matzerath's new assistant. She appears early in 1940, at the end of the period of inactivity known as the "phony war," and with her characteristic brisk competence keeps Oskar supplied with drums throughout the war. Her association with the war, however, is entirely out of her control. She is not a harridan that embodies the spirit of war but a typical Northeast European of country stock with a talent for retailing. In describing her transformation from a roundfaced country girl to the modishly dressed West German subscriber to fashion journals (although she has never been able to disguise her large hands), Grass conveys the change in Germany since the war. A thoroughly normal person and one of Grass' capable female characters, she takes charge of the shop that has been going rapidly downhill since the death of Oskar's mother. Yet it is in this character that recent history, and World War II, is mirrored.

The historical parallel begins with the incidents that revolve around the fizzy lemonade powder (already mentioned in our introductory chapter). Maria is Oskar's first sweetheart, and their adolescent love is represented through the cheap powder which, as we have seen, not only holds sway over their lovemaking but seems to be extended to dominate and color the whole era. A final touch of satire is added when Oskar, finding the powder unobtainable after the war, has some of it prepared in the dispensary of his West German sanatorium. When Maria, now the owner of a small but prospering grocer's shop, comes to visit him, Oskar repeats their grotesque, childish orgy by causing the powder to effervesce in the palm of her hand. The attempt to rouse old-fashioned enthusiasms is, of course, a failure. A shocked Maria, a modern West German to whom former infantile passions are incomprehensible, hastens away from the hospital.

The scene in the sanatorium is one of Oskar's frequent excursions into the contrasting present time. Subsequently, however, he returns to wartime Danzig, sustaining the historical parody. Apparently unaware of what he is doing, Oskar reveals to the reader the beginnings of Maria's rejection of the lemonade powder. Leaving Oskar and his childish love behind her, Maria inevitably seeks out a lover. The pathos of this well-known situation is, in accord with Grass' practice, neglected, whereas the obscene aspect is emphasized. The dominant object now is the chaise longue which saw the lovemaking of Jan Bronski and Oskar's mother. This time it is Matzerath and Maria whom Oskar interrupts—a scene depicted with explicit obscenity.

When Matzerath has departed, enraged by Maria's unpleasant taunts, Maria switches on the radio to listen to a "special announcement" which triumphantly reports German submarine victories in the Atlantic. The juxtaposition is not fortuitous, for Maria's development toward the pleasures represented by the chaise longue parodies that development of history which finds fruition in martial glory. Deeds of war are a matter of public proclamation and acclaim, and their description exerts an irresistible fascination: for this reason Grass first concentrates his readers' attention on the squalid, abject, and inglorious events on the couch and then turns to the "glorious" historical events. The public world of history is trivialized by the parallel with fornication committed by an aging grocer and his young assistant.

At the same time, Grass wittily exposes that double system of values which applies moral standards to sexual matters but displays a strange tolerance in the matter of war—a form of hypocrisy often remarked on, but rarely with such an absolute absence of polemic or indignation. The reader is merely left to observe for himself that it is Matzerath's harmless fornication (he afterwards marries Maria) that makes for passages of gross indecency, while it occurs to no one to attribute a corrupting influence on youth to victory fanfares and special announcements. The chapter closes with tears of pain, rage, and humiliation which, as far as Maria and Oskar are concerned, concern the recently discovered adultery but which the reader more appropriately applies to the large world of the war.

Whereas the chapter, "Special Announcements," concluded in grotesqueness and insanity with Oskar's jealous assault on Maria, the next chapter offers relief in the person of the green-grocer Greff, a highly comic figure in Grass' lower-middle-class portrait gallery and an eccentric described without a trace of bathos. His affected nature lover's language and his vegetarianism arouse the distrust of his stolid North German customers. His attempts to enliven the sobriety of his calling by arranging a device on his potato scales that plays folksongs do nothing to alleviate the suspicions of the local bureau of weights and measures.

Although Greff is generally disliked, it is impossible for the reader to judge whether this dislike is justified or whether it is mere vulgar prejudice against the unusual. In fact, for all the old-fashioned vividness of character portrayal, Greff fits without difficulty into Grass' world. An enthusiastic member of the Scout movement, banned in 1938, and one whose songbook has received official acceptance, he is not a Nazi. His susceptibility to the lean charms of boys indicates degeneracy, although in winter he goes bathing in the ice-bound Baltic and often enjoys a naked romp in the snow with a handful of likely lads.

Greff serves as a witness at the civil wedding of Maria and Matzerath. Oskar's loud assertions that he is the father of the child she is to bear are contradicted by his attempts to induce an abortion by causing Maria to fall (a parallel is drawn with the German parachute attack on Crete) and by stabbing her with scissors. Yet, to the accompaniment of German victories on all fronts, the child is safely delivered and christened. The birth of a son and the few snatches of French that Oskar picks up from the postcards sent by Maria's brother, serving as a soldier in Paris, remind the reader that Oskar's chronicle is a rough parody of the traditional *Entwicklungsroman*. After all, Goethe's Wilhelm Meister, too, has an illegitimate son by the actress Mariane, and traffic with the elegant, civilized world.

The historical and literary parody takes an even more ribald form when Oskar seeks consolation with Greff's wife, a slut who spends her days lounging in an unclean bed. This unwholesome affair runs parallel to the 1941 German campaign in Russia then beginning to get bogged down in mud. The *Entwicklungsroman* is parodied when Oskar says of himself (in the third person) that after his affair with Lina Greff "he could regard his studies as completed" (p. 376). He loftily apologizes for the small shopkeeping milieu in which his education had to be acquired. An encounter with Bebra opens up the opportunity of following Wilhelm Meister's example of completing his education in the theater. Oskar's fellow dwarf is now associated with Goebbels, the Minister of Propaganda, and is accompanied by a midget lady, of vaguely Mediterranean origin, who vainly recalls the mysterious dancing girl, Mignon from *Wilhelm Meister*.

While Oskar is pursuing his education, the world around him shows the first signs of impending collapse. It is September, 1942, and the name "Stalingrad" is mentioned in passing, although only in the form of yet another "special announcement" that the Sixth Army has captured this city. The real meaning of this news is stated in various obscure ways. Greff, for example, hangs himself on a homemade gallows incorporated into his drum-playing potato scales. His suicide marks the disappearance from Oskar's chronicle of the open-air, community-singing aspect of German life. The impending catastrophe takes shape in the threatening emergence of the Black Cook in the children's song, with its refrain "Ist die schwarze Köchin da? – ja, ja, ja!" (p. 388). This song was part of a ritual game of a type common until recent times, which ended, like the English "Oranges and Lemons," with a threat of beheading:

> Dreimal muss sie rummarschieren
> Das vierte Mal den Kopf verlieren.

("She must march round three times, off with her head the fourth time.")

Oskar is only dimly aware of the public events that made 1943 the turning point of World War II. He hears Stalingrad mentioned in a "special announcement," but is more concerned about the fever from which Maria is then suffering. This seems enough, however, to induce Oskar to leave Danzig for a tour of the Western defense system as a member of Bebra's company of entertainers. The dwarf Bebra now wears a captain's uniform and is saluted wherever he goes. It is apparent that propaganda at this stage of the war is all-important as a means of papering over the widening cracks. In an access of classical learning, Oskar recalls Belisarius' hunchback general Narses; he apparently forgets that Belisarius and his generals defeated the Germanic tribes. Oskar's education proceeds apace: he adorns his narrative with French fragments and, to entertain his public, shatters eighteenth-century French glassware instead of coarse German beer bottles with his voice. This final polish is imparted in Paris, which suggests a parallel with the hero of the seventeenth-century picaresque novel *Simplicissimus,* who also encountered the enchantments of the world in Paris before entering on the religious phase of his development.

In April, 1944, with invasion from the West imminent, Bebra's company is sent to the coast of Normandy. This phase of the war is represented by means of a lengthy conversation, much as in the Theater of the Absurd, between members of Bebra's troupe and two soldiers, Corporal Lankes and Lieutenant Herzog, near a concrete gun emplacement, "Dora Seven." At one point in this exchange, the midget Kitty sings a cabaret song whose lyrics express a longing not for the imminent defeat (which, in the customary manner of Grass' characters, everyone knows about but does not discuss), but to the prosperity and coziness awaiting those who survive. The optimistic song recalls the aunt in *Hochwasser* who sews sunshades while the floods are rising. Both serve as a reminder that catastrophe and "normal" life recur independently, it seems, of human intervention. The current catastrophe, however, has not yet run its course, for at the end of the chapter "Mystic, Barbaric, Bored" a shell of the invading armies kills Oskar's friend Roswitha.

An incident that occurs during the visit to the gun emplacement illustrates the suitability of the absurd method for presenting the inconsequential nature of reality. Some nuns appear on the beach before the bunker, gathering shrimps for the children in their crèche. Lieutenant Herzog orders Corporal Lankes to shoot them down. The latter protests that the order is senseless, but when Herzog threateningly insists, Lankes shrugs his shoulders and complies. The whole incident is pointless and devoid of drama. In this spirit, without passion or remorse, war crimes are committed.

Oskar returns to a still undamaged Danzig just in time for Kurt's third birthday on June 12, 1944. Oskar's "son," however, is by now three centimeters taller than his "father" and full of infantile destructiveness. Not only does he prophetically destroy a model of the sailing ship "Pamir" (which, in fact, sank in mid-Atlantic after the War) and a proffered tin drum, but he attacks Oskar with a whip, as though he were a spinning top. The scourging, a confused reference to the Trinity, and the question of double paternity mark Oskar's emergence as a grotesque Messiah. From this chapter, "The Imitation of Christ," to the end when Oskar, at the age of thirty, feels that the time has come for him to gather disciples, the Messiah motif plays an important part in the novel. In this role Oskar can be considered as having reached the peak of such development as his day and age allow him.

Oskar's apotheosis begins when Maria, perhaps because the lengthening casualty lists have made her thoughtful, takes Oskar to the Catholic Church just as his mother had done before the war. On that occasion, the Infant Jesus failed to respond when Oskar hung his drum around the statue's neck. This time, however, the statue not only plays Oskar's drum but appoints Oskar as his successor after he has duly denied him three times. Far from being flattered, Oskar is at first angry that Jesus, not content with the Cross, should now want to usurp his drum. Grass chooses this grotesque anecdote to show his admiration for the ability of the Catholic Church to accommodate irrational forces (namely, the drum), even though official Christianity relegates these to Satan. C. G. Jung insists that the Trinity should really be a Quarternity, incorporating these dark urges of the unconscious; and it is perhaps in recognition of the necessity of this concession to Satan that Oskar, returning home, ceremonially shatters *four* lightbulbs with his voice.[7]

In reality, of course, the whole affair is too trivial to deserve much speculation. The reader of Oskar's chronicle is compelled to observe that his *imitatio Christi* lacks conviction. Many of Oskar's activities have hovered in the borderland between illusion and reality, but now the illusion is wearing thin. The small, private miracle in the church remains unconfirmed, and the statue never stirs again in spite of cold nights spent in the draughty church. Harsh reality is far too insistent to be overlooked. The German armies are retreating on all fronts, and the murderous spirit of the times is reflected in the notices which Matzerath receives, urging him to place Oskar in an asylum in accordance with Nazi health regulations. The nightmare situation arises in which the "child" overhears his "parents" discussing the advisability of his being sent away to be killed in the name of racial hygiene. It is not Oskar's Messianic pose that saves him, or the shadowy figure of Bebra who has completely faded away, but the prosaic fact of Matzerath's good nature and paternal feelings. Maria, on the contrary, a mirror of the times as always, is in favor of having Oskar disposed of. Oskar is prepared, at long last, to admit that Matzerath is his real father.

Oskar, however, cannot exist without illusion. In this and in his persistent infantilism he serves as a substitute for Hitler, the original drummer. In the apocalyptic closing stages of the war, he succeeds in finding a group of disciples—a gang of youths who roam about Danzig raping and plundering. With his farsighted impartiality, Oskar notes the existence of many movements at this time, vastly different in their aims, but all symptomatic of the same decay and expressive of the *Zeitgeist*—the Polish partisans, the conspirators against Hitler, a Communist underground movement among the Danzig dock workers, and such gangs as this which existed in all German cities at the time.

The Danzig gang, whose leader calls himself "Störtebeker"—the name of a fourteenth-century Baltic and North Sea pirate—adopts Oskar as a mascot, because the members are impressed by his glass-shattering voice (displayed in all superfluity, in the middle of an air-raid). Under the proud name of "Jesus," Oskar assumes leadership of the group which breaks off all associations with Communist resistance groups and begins to decorate the group headquarters with ornaments stolen from churches. The whole episode continues the parody of the *Entwicklungsroman*. In his apotheosis, Oskar is attempting to create an ethical Utopia in the tradition of Plato, Thomas More, and the "Pädogogische Provinz" in Goethe's *Wilhelm Meisters Wanderjahre* where a restricted group lives according to principles of wisdom and virtue, bringing up the younger generation in the same spirit.

Oskar induces his gang to give up their looted machine guns: "Our weapons are of another kind" (p. 461). His remoteness from the everyday and his exclusiveness recall the spiritual province of Castalian in Hermann Hesse's 1943 work *Glasperlenspiel* (The Bead Game). Both Goethe and Hesse lay stress on ritual; Oskar and his gang hold a Mass in the church, and he supervises it from a vantage point on the statue of the Virgin Mary where he has replaced the Infant Jesus. For all its elaborate background, the whole scheme comes to nothing. The Black Mass is interrupted by the police, for the gang has been betrayed by Luzie, Störtebeker's slight, pale and ruthless girl friend, who unconcernedly looks on as the police lead them away.

Again Oskar escapes all punishment, for even though he is older than the members of his gang, he outwardly still resembles a three-year-old. The situation is presented in a grotesque parable in which Luzie Rennwand, aided by judges, witnesses, and the general public, encourages each member of the gang, beginning with Störtebeker himself, to jump from a high diving board into a swimming pool without water. All submit to Luzie except Oskar himself who tamely climbs down the ladder. The reader, who until now has regarded Oskar as a leader who deserts his followers, realizes that the parable is open to another interpretation. Oskar can also be regarded as a Christ in the wilderness, resisting Satan who tempts Him to plunge down from a high pinnacle. This reading gains increasing justification when, later in Oskar's account, the whole city of Danzig appears to follow Luzie Rennwand's victims in their death-plunge, as artillery fire destroys the old city street by street. The effect is, as one critic remarks, that of a medieval dance of death.

Luzie Rennwand becomes, from this point of view, a manifestation of the unholy spirit of Danzig history, a successor to the figurehead that kills Herbert Truczinski. Oskar calls her "the flapper who unceasingly murders man," and reports the fear that still haunts him in his West German sanatorium: "Now Luzie Rennwand is coming and, a bugbear and Black Cook, challenges you for the last time to take the plunge" (p. 482). Thus Luzie is associated with both the figurehead and the Black Cook.

Whether or not Oskar's abandonment of his disciples is to be admired, stark reality soon puts a temporary stop to any further activities in this direction. The Russians have by now reached Elbing in nearby East Prussia, and the remaining inhabitants of Danzig take refuge in their cellars. Instead of a parable, a detailed account of the course of the destruction in the old city (the punning style reminds one commentator of a baroque funeral oration) and of the death and burial of Mother Truczinski is given. When Matzerath and others set out with the homemade coffin on a handcart, the streets are crowded with refugees and German tanks retreating from the high ground around Danzig. As a climax of horror, the trees lining the main road—the Hindenburgallee—are weighed down with soldiers, old and young, hanged for "treason," as cardboard signs proclaim.

Oskar looks for his former disciple, but without much hope, for "young fellows all look alike after they've been hanged" (p. 482). The arrival of the Russians, which might have been the climax of the narrative, is treated with the same ironic casualness, even flippancy. Oskar's unconcern suggests that this final catastrophe does not come as a surprise, that it has, in a sense, been expected and even desired. Here again Oskar makes visible a current in German history without pathos or false drama. When Russians enter the cellar where Matzerath and his family are hiding, Oskar prevents his father from disposing of his Party badge. He rescues it from its hiding place and stealthily presses it into Matzerath's hand as the Russians stand nearby. The terrified Matzerath tries to swallow the incriminating object, chokes, and is shot by a nervous Russian. This provides a clear example of the object dominating human activity, without regard for the distinctions between comedy and tragedy, and constitutes a parody of the end of the Third Reich. Oskar has now been responsible for the deaths of two fathers, one Polish and one German, and must be regarded as an unusually uninhibited exponent of what, according to psychoanalysts, is a common masculine urge. The unconstructive purposelessness of his deeds matches recent history and, again, the Expressionist frenzy—for example, that of the fifteen-year-old hero of Arnolt Bronnen's drama *Vatermord* (Parricide).

An excursion through Danzig's bloody history from the time when it was the fishing village of Gyddanycz through numerous invasions by Pomeranians, Teutonic Knights, Saxons, Swedes, French and Prussians—which becomes almost comic in the repetition—leads Oskar to the most recent invasion, the arrival of the Poles on the heels of Rokossovski's troops. One of them, a Jew named Fajngold, takes over Matzerath's house and shop.

This figure exemplifies the prevalent intrusion of the comic into the dreadful, for Fajngold is a man whom suffering has made eccentric. He imagines himself accompanied everywhere by his wife and children, although these were killed in the Treblinka extermination camp. Fajngold himself survived his captivity because he was employed as a disinfector. As a result, he clings to disinfectant as the one stable factor in an uncertain world. He insists on disinfecting, first his imaginary family, then Maria and her son Kurt, and finally Oskar himself who is lying in bed seriously ill. In his fever "borne on a cloud of lysol," Oskar hears Fajngold's story of his life in Treblinka and the revolt of the camp's inmates against their captors. In a chronicle where so much has been grotesque, reality now proves more than adequate in providing fevered visions. Another visitor is a doctor who keeps herself awake by means of chain-smoking cigarettes and constant injections of drugs. She apologizes for falling asleep while examining Oskar, explaining that she has been unable to sleep normally since witnessing the drowning of four thousand East Prussian refugee children. Oskar has a grotesque vision of these children riding on a giant carousel, begging for release, while God the Father, Goethe, and Rasputin remorselessly insist on paying for another round. This Expressionist vision of life as a senselessly cruel merry-go-round which torments its children recalls a similar image in Ernst Toller's drama *Hinkemann* of 1924,[8] which, in its turn, owes much to Georg Büchner and the mountebank scenes in *Woyzeck*. In Grass' novel, the year 1945 is reflected, appropriately enough, in the delirium of a fever patient afflicted by a mysterious ailment of long standing.

The Postwar World

Oskar's illness is a parody of German history. After 1945 he undergoes a kind of rebirth, beginning with the burial of the Nazi Matzerath, when Oskar throws his infantile drum into the grave, telling himself that he should have done so sixteen years ago during his visit to Jan Bronski's grave in the same cemetery. Oskar's achievement of maturity is accompanied by his willingness to face the fact that, rather than the romantic, melancholic Pole Bronski, the prosaic German Matzerath is his true father—plainly an ironic parallel to the relinquishment of the German dream of expansion to the East. Oskar is, in fact, now twenty-one years old, and his coming-of-age is confirmed by much play on this number (recalling similar play on the number thirty-two in *Hundejahre*). Thus, Matzerath's coffin is buried at a depth of 1 meter and 21 centimeters, and when Bruno measures him in West Germany, Oskar is 1 meter and 21 centimeters tall. A return to the present, only apparently fortuitous, allows the reader to observe sardonically that the state of maturity has not been of long duration. Oskar has, in the meantime, resumed his drum, obviously unable to relinquish his aggressiveness.

The process of maturing leaves Oskar weak, feverish, and misshapen, but his growth is not yet complete. He continues to grow on the refugee train from Danzig to the West and reaches his full height in the sanatorium, so that now he is no longer short enough for a circus midget. The maturity that Oskar has gained in his cramped, hygienic ward, which plainly represents West Germany, is gained at the expense of infantile vitality. It is true that he has resumed playing his tin drum, but in the last chapter of the Second Book he is represented as being too feeble to hold it. The chronicle reporting his final departure from Danzig, jumping-off place for far-ranging adventures in the pre-1914 world described at the beginning of the novel, must be completed by his attendant Bruno.

Although Bruno is, we have been told, an entirely different "hero," his style is the same as Oskar's, even though traditional aesthetic theory, which Oskar has so stoutly defended, would demand a variation in point of view and style. Bruno's style, however, remains pure Oskar, and is characterized by the same elaborate hypotactical participles: "In that night died, cursing God loudly and indecently, summoning the working class to the struggle, praising freedom with his last words—just as one hears in the films—and finally succumbing to a fit of vomiting that horrified the whole wagon, the Social Democrat who had been far too closely attached to his single-breasted suit" (p. 528). The style is callously ironic, because in an absurd world irony is the only possible attitude. The Social Democrat, for example, dies, not at the hands of the Nazis, but as the result of a kick delivered by a former Polish partisan wearing heavy German military boots—the symbolic jackboots with which the Wehrmacht had trampled across Poland. In accordance with Grass' usual scheme, the implication is that the real initiative lies not so much with the wearer but with the boots themselves, as it does with Oskar's drum or the figurehead in the Danzig museum.

The journey ends in Düsseldorf, where Oskar is confined to a hospital from August, 1945, until May, 1946. From this point on, the autobiographical elements plays an important part, for Grass, too, after being released from an American prisoner-of-war camp in 1946, settled in Düsseldorf in 1947 to study art at the Academy. Here Grass was reunited with his sister who had found employment as a midwife in the hospital, and Grass was made much of by the nurses. Oskar shares his creator's enthusiasm for nurses, who recur at intervals throughout the chronicle, where their white dresses provide a contrast to the Black Cook and her minions. The Second Book ends with Bruno's report that Oskar has just grown another two centimeters.

On being released from the hospital to begin a new life, Oskar finds Maria and Kurt who have found lodgings with Maria's sister, and are conducting a flourishing black market business, characteristic of the period. For a short time Oskar seeks entertainment in cultural activities equally typical of the immediate postwar period in Germany, but this does not last long. In 1947 he finds employment with Korneff, a maker of monuments. The neighboring yards are owned by C. Schnoog and Julius Wöbel, names which recall the firm of Göbel and Moog for which Grass himself worked as a stonemason while waiting for the Düsseldorf Academy to open. The use of modified names, here and elsewhere, is characteristic of Grass' interweaving of autobiographical elements into his fiction. The author's reading, too, shows itself not only in the parodistic patterns, but in names and places. Erich Maria Remarque's 1956 novel *Der schwarze Obelisk* (The Black Obelisk), for example, contains a monumental mason's yard which employs a salesman named Oskar Fuchs. He has the nickname of "Tear-Oskar" [9] due to his habit of inducing tears in the presence of bereaved customers with the aid of a raw onion. This may well be the source of Grass' farcical Düsseldorf nightclub, the "Onion Cellar."

In spite of its ample details, the postwar section of the novel is, as critics have observed, less satisfactory than the first section set in Danzig. The narrative of the West German Oskar is more consciously grotesque. He cannot help criticizing what he observes, so that the thoughts and feelings have become abstracted from the setting. It is perhaps the awareness of this fact that makes Grass cause his hero to abandon commerce for art in 1949 at a time when everyone else is laying the foundations of West German prosperity.

In 1949 Grass entered the Düsseldorf Academy to learn modeling and drawing under the sculptor Sepp Mages and the painter Otto Pankok, who appear in *Die Blechtrommel* as Maruhn and Kuchen. They employ Oskar as a model in various roles, classical and otherwise. His career reaches its peak, however, when he poses for an artist known as Raskolnikov because he continually mutters of crime and punishment. For him, Oskar resumes his old Messianic role and poses as the Infant Jesus, seated on the lap of Ulla, the girl friend of the former soldier Lankes, now an artist. It is only a matter of time before Raskolnikov, a man of powerful intuitions and plainly a revival of the Rasputin element of Oskar's environment, notices a vacuum between Oskar's hands and provides a drum to fill it. Oskar is gradually resuming his old role, and he greets the foundation of the "Bundesrepublik" equipped with a new drum.

Wishing to enjoy his new independence, Oskar finds a room in a house still standing in the Jülicher Strasse, a name which provides a link with the opening scenes of the novel when it first occurs among

[81]

Oskar's sick-bed reminiscences. At this point a passing reference to Parzival warns the reader that the quest of Oskar, if he is to be considered a modern Knight of the Grail, will end in a hospital ward. It is on a Good Friday that Oskar, like Parzival, prepares for his retreat. The "hermit," the landlord of the house, turns out to be another figure from Grass' portrait gallery of lower-middle-class characters who can, in time of acute housing shortage, allow his boorishness full rein. With obvious satisfaction, he assigns Oskar to a roughly converted bathroom. The fact that a hospital nurse, Sister Dorothea, occupies a room in the same apartment induces Oskar to stay, for, as he explains, just as Parzival was fascinated by the three drops of blood in the snow, so he, Oskar, is bewitched by the red cross.

The keynote of the latter part of the novel, however, is failure. One day Oskar succeeds in slipping into the nurse's room. He crawls into her wardrobe where he falls into an erotic daydream, mingled with reminiscences of the eel-catcher on the mole at Danzig. Past events are recapitulated with deliberate monotony as if the narrator were marking time in the past, unable to advance to the present. There is something here of Heinrich Böll's *Billard um halbzehn* (Billiards at Half-Past Nine) whose characters remain inactive in a monotonous, inherited ritual until they succeed in breaking free. For Oskar, however, there is no release into effective action. A whole comic chapter is devoted to Oskar's unsuccessful attempt to seduce the nurse with the aid of a length of coconut matting and the stimulation provided by its prickly asperity. It is a scene which is tedious in its grotesque impropriety, but it does serve to prove the point that Oskar no longer possesses his prewar dynamic: "When Satan doesn't feel like it, then virtue is triumphant. After all, even Satan may not always feel like it" (p. 641).

But life is not without its compensations. Oskar has struck up friendship with a fellow lodger, Egon Münzer, alias Klepp, whose squalid mode of life Oskar describes with relish. Klepp resembles Greff in being eccentric, yet characteristic of his time and place. Klepp's eccentricity includes, for example, the ability to admire both the British royal family and the Communist Party. He is inconsistent even in his laziness, for Oskar's drum achieves the feat of rousing him from his apathy to form a jazz band.

Thus Oskar follows in the footsteps of his creator as a jazz player in the nightclubs of what remained of the older part of Düsseldorf. A 1952 photograph, published in *Der Spiegel*, shows Grass beating on a scrubbing-board accompanied by a guitarist and a recorder-player named, according to the article, Geldmacher (Klepp's name Münzer [coiner] is a pun on this name). Grass' Düsseldorf experiences are utilized in the chapter on the "Zwiebelkeller" (Onion Cellar), an imaginary nightclub which satirizes the West Germany of the 1950's. Here the guests, rendered stiff and unbending by the daily battle for a prosperous existence, rid themselves of their inhibitions by peeling and dicing onions distributed by the proprietor, Schmuh, as the climax of the evening's entertainment.

In the style of a popular sociologist, or of a sympathetic magazine aunt, Oskar tells farcical stories of the sorrows that afflict the customers who need the release provided by Schmuh's onions. Postwar society, however, is lifeless and hard to rouse. One evening, Schmuh recklessly distributes a second round of onions, but even this extra stimulus fails to bring about a real orgy; it produces merely half-hearted noise. It is not until Oskar plays his drum and thus transports his guests back to prewar Danzig, especially to the "uncanny Gutenberg memorial," that they are really carried away. This is so unpleasant that the members of the audience express their newly discovered animation by losing control of their bladders, drastically indicating their return to childhood.

Not everyone needs the stimulus of Oskar's drum to be made aware of the attractions of the past. Lieutenant Herzog, for example, revisits Normandy to fondle the concrete bunker he had commanded on the invasion coast. Oskar encounters him a second time during a visit to France in company with Lankes. They are living in the bunker when Herzog appears on a private tour of inspection, tries to force his way in, and is knocked down by Lankes. There follows a strange scene, in which the nuns whom Lankes had shot, or possibly their ghosts, appear again on the beach, gathering shells.

Lankes, an interesting minor figure in the novel, is plainly intended to cut across any dramatic conceptions about remorse for war crimes or, on the other hand, about the demonic villainy of war criminals. He is mean, tough, selfish, and brutal, but far from neurotic and not at all addicted to unnecessary bloodshed. Having killed the nuns on orders from his officer, the matter does not trouble him. Left to himself, he would not have shot them. How he would have treated them is shown in a peculiar scene in which he entices the youngest and prettiest nun into the bunker and seduces her. Afterwards he sprawls in the sand, smoking unconcernedly while Oskar, from the top of the bunker, unconsciously parodying the device of teichoscopy, reports on her suicide by drowning. With an artist's detachment, Lankes uses the theme for his paintings, and his success inspires Oskar to public performances with his drum.

Lankes and Oskar represent artistry that owes its inspiration to memories of a barbaric past. The dubious aspect of this situation is reflected in the fact that the head of the agency to whom Oskar applies for concert engagements is none other than Bebra, the war-time propagandist now providing peacetime entertainment. Further-more, Oskar emphasizes that his drumming is popular not so much among young jazz enthusiasts as among members of the older gen-eration. They, Oskar insists, want to revive the exhilaration of their youth when grandpapa was, so to speak, a reckless bandit chieftain and grandmama his bride—again the *Hochwasser* theme of people looking back to catastrophe not without longing. Here, too, is the suggestion—developed in *Hundejahre*—that hope lies in the genera-tion uncorrupted by the past. The fact that Oskar finds Bebra in an agency called "West," which he chooses in preference to a possibly existing agency "East," reflects a certain preparedness to consider the East German claim that their regime is free from "revanchist" tendencies.

"Revanchism" and failure to overcome the past are the themes of a grotesque episode in which Oskar and his friend Gottfried von Vittlar go for a joyride in a stolen streetcar. The car is stopped by two men in green hats. They are leading to execution a certain Victor Weluhn, a defender of the Danzig Polish Post Office in 1939, who had managed to escape just before the Germans entered the building. One of the escorts has a crumpled death warrant issued by the Nazi authorities, and he still considers it valid in Western Germany. There are even tentative hints at a piece of semi-humorous sym-bolism in which the streetcar stands for Western Germany, for while the authorities know nothing of this unauthorized journey to the place of execution, they do unwittingly supply the current. Weluhn is rescued from his executioners by a squadron of Polish Uhlans riding soundlessly over the moonlit cabbage patches on the outskirts of Düsseldorf.

From the very beginning of his chronicle, Oskar has been reticent about the reason for his confinement under the watchful eye of an attendant, although early in the first chapter he mentions visits from a lawyer. Now, toward the end of the Third Book, the missing pieces are supplied in a kind of parodied detective mystery. The first indica-tions are vague and cautious. We hear that Oskar had rented Sister

Dorothea's room in the lodging house after his unsuccessful assault on her. Although he tells us that the room is unoccupied, he does not say what has happened to her. He does explain, however, that Klepp has left to get married. In his loneliness, Oskar goes walking with a (hired) dog in the country near Düsseldorf. The dog disappears into a field of rye, to reappear shortly afterwards with an object in its mouth, which it insists on presenting to Oskar. On closer inspection, it turns out to be a woman's finger, complete with ring; as often in Grass, the impression is gained of Germany as a land thickly strewn with corpses. As one of the lunatics in Peter Weiss' *Jean Paul Marat* puts it:

> In meinem jahrtausendlangen Leben
> war ich an Millionen von Morden beteiligt
> Dick gedüngt
> Dick gedüngt ist überall die Erde
> vom Brei der menschlichen Eingeweide.[10]

("In my thousand-year-long life I took part in millions of murders. The earth is everywhere thickly dunged with human guts.")

The whole scene with the finger has been witnessed by Gottfried von Vittlar from his vantage point in an apple tree, and the narrative continues for a time in the form of his statement to a court of justice in which Oskar is referred to as "the accused." Oskar, it turns out, is charged with the murder of Sister Dorothea. Although, with comic punctilio, Vittlar refuses to express an opinion on Oskar's guilt, he feels obliged to report highly suspicious circumstances, including Oskar's habit of worshipping the finger preserved in a jar of spirits.

The chapter reporting the finding of the finger, "The Last Streetcar, or Worship of a Preserving Jar," is contrived so as to create a parallel to the earlier chapter "He Lies in Saspe" which reports Oskar's visit to Jan Bronski's grave after his execution. In both chapters, aircraft take off from a nearby field; in both there appears a letter signed by Feldjustizinspektor Zelewski, announcing the execution of a defender of the Polish Post Office. In both chapters, too, the gallant Polish cavalry appears; in the early chapter, the cavalry quixotically attacks German tanks; in the later, it rescues Weluhn from execution. The comforting figures of hospital nurses and vaguely symbolic streetcars recur on both occasions.

In fact, very few positive changes have taken place since Oskar's

Danzig days—a melancholy truth which is reflected in the final chapter, "Thirty," on the plane of Oskar's private life. Thirty is an important age in the development of the hero. As Vittlar points out, it was at this age that Christ gathered disciples and embarked on his mission. Ingeborg Bachmann recognizes the importance of this age in her volume of prose pieces, *Das dreissigste Jahr* (The Thirtieth Year). Oskar, however, wishes to spend his adult life in his little white bed in the sanatorium, his chief fear being that his case may be reopened, his innocence established, and he would have to leave his snug berth.

Oskar's life, like that of Adrian Leverkühn in *Doktor Faustus*, runs parallel to the course of German history. Leverkühn's insanity, however, linked to the narrator's account of the death agonies of the Third Reich, arouses pity and fear. Oskar's insanity, on the other hand, is that of a petulant child. It is not a final catastrophe but a retreat into a hygienic refuge. As the story approaches its end, which will leave Oskar where we found him in the beginning, he recalls his flight to Paris two years previously when the train wheels repeated the nursery rhyme ("Ist die schwarze Köchin da, ja, ja, ja . . .") which brings back his childhood fears and confirms his decision to seek refuge. He is arrested on the escalator of a Paris metro station, ascending towards heaven at an angle of 45°, a fact which encourages him to announce in three languages to the detectives, "I am Jesus!" The novel ends, then, in a triple climax: the arrest of the murderer, as in a detective story; the peak of development as in the "Entwicklungsroman"; and, finally, the retirement to a hermitage favored by the picaresque novel. For all its thunder, however, it is a false climax because Oskar takes leave of his readers by singing the nursery rhyme of the threatening Black Cook whom all the white-robed attendants in his sanatorium cannot drive away. It is apparent that the Black Cook, in various guises, has accompanied him throughout and that, even if children no longer sing of her, she continues to haunt Oskar.

CHAPTER 5

Katz und Maus (Cat and Mouse)

*D*IE *Blechtrommel* was followed in 1961 by *Katz und Maus,* a novelle or long short story, representing a genre which has played an important part in German literature.

Grass has used the novelle form as a means of disciplining his inventiveness, chiefly through manipulation of the point of view. On the surface, *Katz und Maus* has much in common with *Die Blechtrommel.* Both works contain a variety of grotesque episodes set against a minutely observed petit-bourgeois background of prewar Danzig. In both, the main character is deformed and eccentric. In *Katz und Maus* it is the schoolboy Mahlke, who has an oversized Adam's apple and wears a variety of objects on a string around his neck. The perspective from which the events are observed, however, makes the two works very different from each other. In the novel, the point of view is Oskar's, who observes Danzig society. It is a scurrilous, worm's-eye view of a broad field of activity—far too broad a field for the purposes of the novella. In the novella the eccentric central character is the focus of attention. He is observed from the point of view of the narrator, who is not himself an important figure. In his lack of comprehension of the hero, the narrator Pilenz, a school friend, is, however, a representative of the society in which both move, although no one (except the reader) really grasps this fact. In *Die Blechtrommel,* then, we look at society from the point of view of an individual, with a consequent dispersal of attention, whereas in the novella, society—through the narrator—looks at an individual, thus giving the author a better chance to impose form and pattern on his material. Whereas the events in *Die Blechtrommel* roughly tag along behind the historical events, the plot of *Katz und Maus* reaches a turning point in Chapter VII, the central chapter, when Mahlke attends a lecture given by the submarine commander, which leades to Mahlke's clash with the authorities.

Mahlke's actions reveal him as a true hero with the hero's traditional attributes of bravery, honesty, modesty, and chastity. As Dostoevsky has pointed out, there is nothing more difficult than to portray a positively good man! [1] Grass deploys all his arts to convince the reader of a virtuous hero who, without being priggish, asserts his qualities in the moral pig-sty of everyday life. Grass succeeds in this aim, thanks partly to his device of a narrator who, only dimly aware of the hero's virtues, is constantly aware of the ridiculous figure he cuts. The reader is never allowed to forget Mahlke's immense Adam's apple, the "mouse" of the title and a constant reminder that Mahlke is different from his fellows and in danger of being victimized. The choice of this particular deformity is not, of course, pure fancy. The Adam's apple, which the narrator and society find merely ridiculous, is that piece of the forbidden fruit which Adam could not succeed in swallowing, and thus a suitable symbol of innocence. The biblical apple resembles the repulsive food appearing elsewhere in Grass' works in that it is a cipher for the unpalatable world which unfortunate mankind cannot easily swallow.

Further meaning is given to the experiences of the central character by means of parallels with established mythical and literary patterns. The reader is allowed to glimpse fleeting resemblances between Mahlke, on the one hand, and Parzival, King Arthur, and Dostoevsky's Holy Fool, on the other. There is even a vague suggestion of a link between Mahlke's final disappearance and the fall of Danzig in the last stages of the Second World War. Had Danzig been able to appreciate Mahlke's virtues, the fall might have been averted. As we have seen, the same device of coyly hidden references is used in *Die Blechtrommel* as a kind of generalized irony. In *Katz and Maus,* the fact that the narrator fails to see these parallels gives added point to the irony.

We learn of the events through the distorting medium of a narrator who has no real understanding of Mahlke's virtues, although he finds himself inexplicably fascinated by him. The real significance of the central character, however, is nowhere explicitly stated. In the general press of business, the first critics and commentators failed to show a real understanding of Mahlke, although there are signs that this situation is improving. The critics, like Pilenz, were fascinated but could not say why. The commentators were inclined to find the obscenity offensive and lacking in thematic justification. An exception was Hans Magnus Enzensberger, who observed that the cat of the title represents the society in which Mahlke, the "mouse," lives.[2] Herbert Ahl admires the compactness of this novella,[3] while other critics, e.g. Wilhelm Duwe,[4] can see only a falling-off from *Die Blechtrommel.*

So much disagreement calls for closer examination of the text. The opening scene immediately disposes of the charge of random grotesqueness or pointless obscenity. At the very outset, Mahlke is presented in a posture significant for the whole story, that of a martyr. He is one of a group of schoolboys lying in the grass at the edge of a playing field, when some unknown hand, presumably that of the narrator, sets a cat on to Mahlke's "mouse." The narrator, Pilenz, is among the group of Mahlke's tormentors, a clear warning, on the threshold of the story, that we should read between the lines of his account. Such small-scale martyrdom is continued throughout the novella. Mahlke does not become a leader of the elite "Jungvolk," as do most of his classmates in the highly regarded *Gymnasium*, but joins the Hitler Youth—"a slovenly organization, where people like Mahlke could submerge" (p. 31). ("Submerge" is later to acquire ironic significance.)

One of Mahlke's schoolmates, a smart young aristocrat from the Baltic states, draws an effective caricature of Mahlke, with his hair parted in the middle, his receding chin, and his prominent "mouse," adding to his long-suffering expression the Savior's halo—again a tacit hint at Mahlke's true status. The martyrdom reaches its climax when Mahlke is refused permission to deliver the customary lecture in his old school, the so-called *Conradinum* in Danzig, after he has been decorated with the Ritterkreuz. It is then that Mahlke recognizes that in a strange way he is at odds with society.

Grass is careful not to make Mahlke's martyrdom synonymous with weakness or priggishness. The first chapter begins in a puzzling way: "And once, when Mahlke could already swim, we were lying in the grass near the stadium." We soon learn the significance of this. Mahlke first swam at the age of fourteen, but once he learned, he excelled all the other boys. It was at this time that his Adam's apple developed. With a screwdriver hung around his neck, he engages in salvaging from the wrecked Polish minesweeper lying in Danzig bay—feats that arouse the admiration of his friends. The prominent Adam's apple that sets him apart as an innocent martyr is, at the same time, a sign of manhood. Mahlke is not only mentally but also physically more mature than his companions. The screwdriver and other objects that hang around his neck have a phallic significance that Grass genially but firmly insists on. One obscene episode in particular underlines Mahlke's strength and heroism from this aspect. The boys who have swum out to the minesweeper pass the time in masturbation. Tulla, a small girl prominent in *Hundejahre*, is present as a fascinated spectator and urges Mahlke to take part. Mahlke refuses at first, slapping Tulla's face when she becomes overly insistent. Finally, tired of childish discussion, he joins the others in their infantile orgy and astounds them all. The whole tasteless episode is told with some artistry. The various stages of the action correspond to the movements of ships of various sizes and speeds in the bay. As a reminder of Mahlke's qualities, the ships recur, like a refrain, throughout the story. The episode caused a short-lived scandal on account of its alleged obscenity. The authorities in the German province of Hessen wanted the book declared unsuitable for young people, and this threat caused eminent writers and scholars to hasten to its defense.

Apart from its psychological truth, the incident serves to demonstrate Mahlke's truly heroic ability to establish his virtues in the real world on its own terms. The children in *Katz und Maus* eat seagulls' droppings scraped from the rusty deck of the minesweeper. Mahlke has no part in this. Instead, on one occasion, he dives deeper than anyone else could dive, and salvages a can of frogs' legs, which he consumes to the horror and admiration of them all. This is the kind of bravery that Mahlke's schoolmates can understand and appreciate, even if the school authorities, who believe that virtue should be priggish, do not. He has, in fact, precisely the virtues that befit a fifteen-year-old schoolboy. Pilenz tells us that he was a reasonably good scholar, and then proceeds: "But [he was] no swot, worked only moderately hard, allowed anyone to copy from him, was no tell-tale, developed no special ambition except in gymnastics, had an obvious distaste for the usual disgusting habits of fifteen-year-old schoolboys" (p. 28). This last virtue, already transcending the usual, is concretely illustrated in a disgusting practical joke to be played on a purblind teacher but which Mahlke, calmly and without saying a word, averts at the last moment. His compassionate motives escape his companions, but Mahlke acquires a special reputation, "not good, not bad, a legendary reputation" (p. 31).

The legendary reputation is far more justified than Mahlke's fellows recognize. The narrator is unaware of certain parallels between Mahlke and heroic and saintly figures in myth and literature which are visible to the attentive reader. Like Wolfram von Eschenbach's Parzival, Mahlke has also lost his father in heroic death. He lives with his mother who gives him such strange clothes to wear that he looks comical. When Parzival sets out on his adventures, his mother dresses him in the clothes of a fool. The parallel with Parzival explains Mahlke's wish to become a clown, which he often expresses in the story. After the hero's final disappearance, the narrator searches for him in circuses. The disappearance itself is mysterious and leaves lingering hopes of survival, like that for King Arthur and other mythical heroes. But the comparison with Parzival must not be taken too far. As Oskar remarks in *Die Blechtrommel:* "Do you know *Parzival?* I don't know it especially well, either" (p. 393).

The clown motif, Mahlke's constantly stressed ridiculous appearance, and the strange trembling remarked on by the narrator recall Dostoevsky's epileptic, virtuous idiot, Prince Myshkin. Dostoevsky draws parallels between his hero and Christ just as Grass sometimes compares Mahlke to "der Erlöser" (the Savior, Redeemer). This parallel is not too far-fetched. Grass actually directs the reader to it by means of a reference to Dostoevsky (and to Kierkegaard) which Mahlke makes on his return from the Russian front. Although Mahlke has deserted from the army, and he and Pilenz are looking for a likely hiding place, Mahlke finds time to remark: "I am reading quite a lot of Kierkegaard at present. You really must read Dostoevsky sometime, when you are in Russia. That will make a lot of things clear to you—the mentality and so forth" (p. 156).

The aristocratic knight is traditionally the arbiter of taste. Mahlke, too, performs this function. In his anxiety to hide his Adam's apple, he develops during the third year of the war what he calls "Puscheln" —a kind of necktie consisting of two tassels of wool connected by a thread. The fashion is eagerly taken up by the other schoolboys and sweeps across Germany (it's existence is a matter of historical fact). The significant aspect of this affair is that it brings Mahlke into conflict with the school authorities who apparently understand him even less than do his companions. *Oberstudienrat* Klohse forbids the fashion as unwarlike and unworthy of German youth.

As a leader of fashion, Mahlke is successful and misunderstood. This applies even more strongly to his exercise of the knightly virtue of chastity; but, then, who understands chastity? The narrator, who is as confused as anyone else, expresses the tentative opinion that Mahlke, the clown, is helpless in the presence of girls: "He stared at my girl cousins from Berlin like a fish. If at all, then he was more for boys: not that I mean he was queer" (p. 43). What emerges from all this contradiction is a grotesque anecdote that demonstrates to the perceptive reader that Mahlke, as a true knight, is attractive to women, and yet chaste.

The narrator and a friend named Schilling take the sophisticated Berlin cousins for a walk across the frozen sea to the minesweeper in the hope of impressing the visitors from the capital. At the wreck they meet Mahlke who is trying to bore a hole in the ice above the hatchway that gives access to the interior of the ship. Against all expectations, the girls are greatly impressed by the shabby figure. They address Mahlke respectfully as "Sie" and "Herr Mahlke," while Pilenz and Schilling are reduced to the status of small boys with running noses. In fact, the girls are so impressed that they volunteer to urinate on the ice in order to aid Mahlke in his task. Under Mahlke's influence, the whole affair is conducted with rigid propriety —the boys look away. For the remainder of their visit, and to the irritation of the other two boys, the girls talk only about Mahlke. Meanwhile, Mahlke has bored a hole at the spot where he wants it, exactly above the hatchway, although there is no one to applaud his skill.

The fact is, however, Pilenz goes on to explain, Mahlke has an audience, the only one he cares about: the Virgin Mary. The jump from the Berlin cousins to this subject is not gratuitous. Mahlke has succeeded in finding an outlet for adolescent sexuality in this traditional, knightly way. Grass characteristically drives Mahlke's position to the extreme of caricature by turning, through the words of of the priest Gusewski, his worship of Mary into a heathen cult. Thus, he erects a chapel in Mary's honor in the radio operator's cabin of the minesweeper, accessible to him alone because the entrance lies far below water level. Only when he is kneeling before her image in church does he bare his Adam's apple, a symbol of martyrdom and maturity.

Mahlke's cult of Mary is relevant to another important motif that arises from his heroic qualities, namely his unconscious opposition to the society in which he lives. Toward the end, before his final disappearance, he says: "Of course I don't believe in God. The usual swindle to cheat the people. The only one I believe in is the Virgin Mary. That's why I will never get married (p. 156). The rejection of a male god implies Mahlke's rejection of a society, dominated by a solitary male figure, in which harsh masculine values prevail. Another aspect of the cult is given in his first great find in the remote depths of the Polish minesweeper—a medallion with "the famous

Matka Boska Czestochowska," a Madonna of the officially despised Poles. *Oberstudienrat* Klohse, the principal of Mahlke's school and Mahlke's consistent enemy, later forbids him to wear the Polish article around his neck in school. With his unfailing instinct for what is proper, Mahlke hangs up the medallion between a medal depicting the Polish hero Pilsudski and a postcard showing the hero of the German campaign in Norway. Mahlke's refusal to conform to the official German attitude toward the Poles receives more attention later in the story.

At this stage, the real test of Mahlke's virtues comes in his encounter with the official attitudes to World War II raging outside. This clash takes the altogether natural form of attendance at two lectures arranged by the school authorities and given by former pupils of the *Conradinum* who have distinguished themselves in action. The first lecturer is a fighter pilot who has shot down over forty enemy aircraft (apparently *not* a theme which could endanger the morals of young people). He has been congratulated by Hitler personally and has been awarded a medal which, German style, is suspended on a ribbon worn around the neck just like Mahlke's trophies.

The lieutenant is appropriately modest about his achievements. Grass has never believed in simplifying reality. Yet there is an inherent falsity about his tone, and Grass knows how to reveal it. The lieutenant is a little too ready to demonstrate with his hands and to mention the *Kasino* (Officers' Mess) in his lecture. His concluding remarks strike a theatrical note: "Lads, take it from me, when you are out there in action, you start thinking a lot about your schooldays" (p. 63). The children applaud enthusiastically, and *Oberstudienrat* Klohse rises in a whiff of peppermint to utter a string of empty patriotic exhortations about being clean and hard. Grass renders this speech by running together incomplete clichés and propaganda slogans with the air of one who is too weary to trouble finishing them. Mahlke does not applaud with the rest. He has observed the medal adorning the lieutenant's neck and is envious.

This envy leads to a period of depression and inactivity—a phase through which saints and heroes usually pass. Mahlke does no more diving but simply swims across to the minesweeper and lounges on the deck. The inactivity is interrupted (again in accord with the heroic tradition) by the need for the hero's services:—he must come to the rescue of a small boy trapped in the wreckage. Thus prompted, Mahlke resumes his activities more daringly than ever. He dives and remains absent for so long that his friends, believing him drowned, discuss making a collection for a wreath. Mahlke has over-heard these rumors of his premature martyrdom; and they hear him laughing from the interior of the wreck. He emerges from the hatch-way, cackling in a fashion "good-natured rather than contemptuous." He has gained access to the wireless cabin of the ship and proceeds to establish his private quarters there, complete with pictures of the Virgin Mary. His heroism has entered a new and higher phase. He is heard intoning the "Stabat Mater" from the interior of the wreck, and he begins to return all the booty he has acquired, includ-ing the phonograph on which he once played religious music. It is plain that he is on the verge of great deeds, and his companions, sensing this, speak of his "sore throat" ("er hat wieder Halsschmer-zen")—army jargon for an ambitious soldier anxious to win a medal.

The next stage of Mahlke's activities is occasioned by the visit of another war hero to the school. This time it is a U-Boat commander who has sunk a great amount of enemy tonnage. Through a "softly curving speaking-mouth" (weichgeschwungener Sprechmund) he holds forth in dreadful passages of sinister purple prose: "Dazzling white, the froth of the wake, a luxuriously billowing lacy garment, follows the vessel that draws nigh her death-bringing nuptials like a bride festively clad" (p. 83). After the lecture he asks to be allowed to join the boys in the gymnasium. In the locker room he is sur-rounded by eagerly questioning admirers. While he is in the gym-nasium showing off his agility, Mahlke seizes the opportunity to steal the commander's medal which he has been regarding enviously all through the lecture. When the loss is discovered, there ensues a scene of accomplished farce which reveals the weakness of the au-thorities. The teacher in charge violently assaults an innocent by-stander, while the commander betrays increasing nervousness and finally leaves in a thoroughly bad temper to scour Danzig for a *Ritterkreuz* to replace the lost one. The incident has revealed him as one of the hollow men.

Soon afterwards, Mahlke confesses the theft to *Oberstudienrat* Klohse, who seizes the chance to expel him from the *Conradinum*, whereupon Pilenz loses contact with him during the summer of 1942. With Mahlke's disappearance, we hear the first vague rumblings of national catastrophe in the form of the activities of youthful ma-rauders led by one Störtebeker. This group, which plays an impor-tant part in *Die Blechtrommel*, gains real prominence in the final days of Danzig, when the Russian armies are approaching the city at the time of Mahlke's final disappearance. It is not chance that Mahlke's actions are linked with such far-reaching events, but a token of the hero's greatness. Again, it is only apparently by chance that Pilenz introduces the episode of name-changing at this point in the story.

In the early 1940's, when the German cause was apparently prospering, many people with Polish-sounding names had them altered in favor of German ones. Thus the priest Gusewski becomes Gusewing, and the butcher Olczewski calls himself Ohlwein. The name Mahlke, too, ending in -ke, is Polish, although not as obviously so as the others, which end in -ki or -a. Needless to say, Mahlke does not change his name. Neither the priest nor the butcher, with a name neither German nor Polish, he can avoid extremes. This is a sign of his unpretentious matter-of-factness, absence of display, and unselfconscious greatness. The approaching catastrophe shows that the society in which Mahlke lives rejects the qualities he represents at its own peril. All this, it must be emphasized, is presented in hints and implications; Grass does not preach but arranges his materials in such a way as to make certain conclusions possible.

When, after an interval, the narrator next meets Mahlke, now attending a different school, the latter is praying fervently before a statue of the Virgin. Mahlke mentions that he has volunteered for military service and is himself puzzled by his action: "You know how little I think of it all—military war games and this overstressing of the soldierly" (p. 115). It is apparent that this scene in church represents a vigil before going into battle.

Shortly before Christmas, Pilenz visits Mahlke in his home, taking with him a candle (as to the shrine of a saint), and candles were difficult to obtain in those days of severe rationing. During the visit Mahlke is appropriately saintly and, as usual, faintly ridiculous. Mahlke's mother and aunt try to quiz Pilenz about the latest love affair of his mother whose husband is in army service. Mahlke is firm: "Leave it be, aunty. Who is going to act as a judge in times like these, when everything is more or less out of joint" (p. 121).

There follows the climax of Mahlke's career—the bravery that leads to the award of the *Ritterkreuz*. The first intimation of this heroism is inextricably bound up with farce. Mahlke's aunt meets Pilenz in the street and asks him to decipher a letter she has just received from her nephew. It contains a clumsy drawing of Russian tanks, each neatly marked at a point just under the turret. Pilenz condescendingly explains that Mahlke must have destroyed the number of tanks indicated. Mahlke's aunt knows this already; however what puzzles her is the fact that the number of tanks varies from letter to letter. In one letter there were only eight tanks, while the preceding letter listed twenty-seven. "Perhaps," she concludes in her broad dialect and with her own peculiar logic, "it's because the mail deliveries are so irregular" (p. 131).

When the narrator himself is drafted into the army, he finds everywhere traces of the Great Mahlke. "Stabat Mater" is carved boldly into the wooden beams of a latrine, dominating the obscene scrawls. An old soldier has numerous tales of Mahlke's exploits before he was transferred to the front: he had cuckolded a bullying *Oberfeldmeister* and discovered a partisan ammunition dump, among other things.

But for all his heroism, Mahlke retains his role of mouse to the world's cat. His old, instinctive enemy, *Oberstudienrat* Klohse, not only will not permit him to lecture at his old school, but he refuses permission with a detestable, quiet satisfaction. Unconsoled by other offers, Mahlke deserts, is rowed across to the minesweeper, and is never seen again, disappearing mysteriously in the manner of a legendary hero. Danzig falls and Pilenz loses his records and documents during the retreat.

Mahlke disappears because he comes to realize that his qualities are not cherished in the doomed society in which he lives. The decription he gives of his proposed lecture makes this plain. Instead of the submarine commander's quasi-religious mysticism, with the U-Boat gliding to its "death-bringing nuptials," Mahlke wants to begin with a short technical account of tank warfare. (The reader is treated to part of this matter-of-fact material in a talk with a group of schoolboys conducted in the rain.) But, as Mahlke explains, he does not want to talk only about himself. He wants to go on to say a few words about the exploits of his father, an engineer on the Polish railways, who, together with his Polish stoker, lost his life averting a serious accident. What Mahlke, in his innocence, fails to realize is that the authorities do not wish to hear an unpretentious tale of civilian heroism in peacetime Poland. They want their charges to hear flamboyant and bloody deeds of war extolling the glory of the German nation at the expense of its enemies. *Oberstudienrat* Klohse is not interested in true heroism; hence his rejection of Mahlke. To the narrator the whole matter is just another example of Mahlke's eccentricity.

Katz und Maus (Cat and Mouse)

After the War, Pilenz searches for Mahlke everywhere in Western Germany, but without success. Grass' distrust of the *Bundesrepublik* (whether justified or not) is neatly expressed in the vain search for Mahlke at a meeting of the holders of the *Ritterkreuz* held in Regensburg in 1959. The account is superior to the lengthy satire at the end of *Hundejahre* with its grotesque exposures of former Nazis in leading positions. Here the reader is simply left to gather that postwar Germany, too, fails to offer a refuge to a hero of Mahlke's qualities.

All the elements of the story are employed to heighten the significance of the central figure, even the lower-middle-class background. As it does in Grass' novels, this background sets the tone of the era and lends credibility to the grotesqueness of the events, which is less extreme here than in the novels. But there is more to it than this. Consider the name of Mahlke's unpretentious street—Osterzeile. "Oster" suggests "Easter," and thus Mahlke's role as Savior, Redeemer, and Holy Fool. It also suggests "East" and Mahlke's Polish origins. When the narrator first mentions Mahlke's house, he is not sure whether it is in the Osterzeile or in another street called "Westerzeile," a fact which suggests the position of Mahlke (and Danzig) between Germany and Poland, and the opportunity for conciliation he represents.

Much of the surface of this story, the visible action, is deliberately trivial or (as in the case of Mahlke's military career) perfunctorily told. It is perhaps for this reason—the necessity of reading between the lines—that the much-heralded film was not very successful, even though it was the subject of much controversy.[5] Franz-Joseph Strauss, now the West German Finance Minister, objected before the *Bundestag* to certain scenes. The role of Mahlke, incidentally, was acted by the two sons of Willy Brandt, formerly the Socialist Mayor of Berlin and now the West German Vice-Chancellor. Mahlke is at the center of a system of references difficult to convey by means of the cinema.

CHAPTER 6

Hundejahre (Dog Years)

PUBLISHED in 1963, Grass' novel *Hundejahre* has the circular structure familiar from *Die Blechtrommel*. It begins, as it ends, in postwar Western Germany, after a fruitless, absurd excursion through the twelve years of Hitler's Third Reich—twelve years that correspond both in length and in quality to the "dog's life" suggested by the title.

The novel, however, has its starting point not only in Western Germany, but in German, and even European, history. In the opening "First Shift," Brauxel, the owner of a mysterious mine which employs 134 persons but produces neither potash nor coal, is reminiscing about the region at the mouth of the River Vistula. He recalls its varied past that includes floods, alterations in course, religious disputes (between Mennonites and Catholics, for example), wars, legendary heroes, and strange Balto-Slav gods. The novel ends, some six hundred pages later, with fragments of German history enacted by scarecrows in Brauxel's mine deep underneath Western Germany.

History and the flux of time are represented by the river which carries the debris of history, the blood, clay, and ashes of, for example, the Napoleonic siege of Danzig. A flood threatens, caused by mice in the dike. This is a piece of folklore which occurs in many stories of the Northern coasts, including Theodor Storm's *Der Schimmelreiter*. In the Vistula area, the Mennonite fishermen are apt to claim that the Polish Catholics placed the mice there. This brings in its train a whole host of legends which pour like a flood through the breached dike. The novel that follows is, so to speak, part of this flood, so that Hitler's Germany is a grotesque fragment borne along with the other flotsam. The opening scene of *Hundejahre* bears an obvious resemblance to the Liffey passage at the end of the first part of *Finnegans Wake*. Both Joyce and Grass use the river to draw attention to the formless flow of time, which is the raw material with which the narrative must cope.

Among the numerous legendary and historical figures that populate Brauxel's Vistula recurs the "robber Bobrowski" and his companion Materna "from whom everything is derived" (p. 10). In this veiled way Grass makes acknowledgment to the poet Johannes Bobrowski (1917–1965), born in East Prussia, whose poetry and stories conjure up East European landscapes, real and yet visionary, somewhat in the manner of the Wales of Dylan Thomas.[1] More specifically, the Vistula region of pre-1919 West Prussia is the subject of Bobrowski's only novel, *Levins Mühle*[2] (Levin's Mill), set in the village of Neumühl in 1874. The stylistic and thematic similarities between Grass and Bobrowski point to a close mutual influence. Generally speaking, both *Hundejahre* and *Levins Mühle* combine an occasional incantatory style with precise geographical delineation. The local background in both lays stress on the religious antagonism among Protestants, Catholics, and Jews and on the eccentricities of the Mennonites. In both books a mill is burned down out of hatred (Levin's mill is a water mill; Matern's, a wind mill), a christening is a focal event, and gypsies and the cry of a bird are used as recurring background motifs. In Bobrowski's posthumously published prose work *Boehlendorff und Mäusefest* (1965), there appears a black dog called "Perun," the Slav name of the thunder god; in *Hundejahre*, the dog Perkun, bearing the corresponding Baltic name, is the sire of Senta.

Both Grass and Bobrowski digress into history to explain the present. The robber's companion Materna in *Hundejahre* corresponds to Mattern, a minor figure in *Levins Mühle*. Mattern is a Polish highwayman, the narrator's ancestor, who lived by plundering the transport wagons of Danzig merchants, whereas Walter Matern, the modern descendant of Polish robbers, wavers between the Catholic faith of his ancestors and the Nazi Party. Matern (the name is stressed on the final syllable) is introduced in the "First Shift" on the dike near Nickelswalde as he watches the debris float past on the flooded Vistula.

The vagaries of the Vistula—constantly subject to floods in spite of elaborate dikes—reflect the fluidity of the historical situation that characterizes this border region. Brauxel himself shares this impermanence; for the opening sentences show uncertainty not only as to who should act the part of narrator, but even as to the spelling of his name. Brauxel, or Brauksel—later to emerge as Amsel, or Goldmäulchen—is a suitable chronicler for a river which the Germans call "Weichsel" and the Poles call "Wisla," and which becomes broader in the memories of exiles.

An astrological motif is introduced with Brauxel's ironic inquiry: "Should we wait until the eight planets conjugate in the sign of Aquarius?" There is a threat here, residing in the astrological belief that the world, as it passes through the Zodiacal Year of 26,000 years, will move in the year 2000 A.D. from the present age of Pisces into that of Aquarius. A fish is the symbol of Christ, and the age now ending is the age of Christ. The coming age, which is already casting its shadow before it, will reject the doctrine of compassion.

As if to illustrate this, the "Second Shift" opens with Walter Matern, the future persecutor, standing on the mouse-ridden dike, characteristically grinding his teeth. His companion, friend, and future victim is Eddi Amsel, playing with the clothes and sticks washed up by the river. In an accumulation of nameless fury that extends over three sections, Matern seizes a pocket-knife, (a present from Amsel), and flings it into the river. The narrator dives back into time, to Matern's grandmother and beyond, presumably in his search for an explanation; for Grass' world resembles that of Jean Paul in the existence of associations which link apparently disconnected matters. The exploration of the past leads back to the Napoleonic siege of Danzig and to the occasion when Queen Luise of Prussia slept at the Materns' windmill after Napoleon's victory over her armies (an incident mentioned in *Hochwasser*). Even the dog has an ancestry which extends back to a Lithuanian, Russian, or Polish she-wolf.

The narrator finally settles in 1917, the year of Matern's birth, to which the fictional perspective lends an air of extreme remoteness. Matern's grandmother, we are told, has been confined to her chair for nine years as the result of a blow received from her Protestant daughter-in-law. She had accused her daughter-in-law of harboring a mouse in her womb to prevent her presenting the Materns with an heir. The parlor over the kitchen, where she spends her days, is described with a minuteness and with an effect of illuminated stillness—a Dutch interior that conveys the Dutch element in the landscape, temper, and dialect of the region.

Subsequent events disprove the grandmother's folklore. Walter Matern is born and, in her joy, the old lady jumps up from her chair. Or if it is not joy, the miracle is occasioned by her wish to best the half-witted maid servant who is burning the goose provided for the christening feast. The grandmother's leap is accompanied by other phenomena: stove tiles crack, lettuce leaves wither, a tortoise dies, and her chair crumbles to dust. On behalf of the reader, Brauxel asks whether all these extravagant stage effects are necessary. Why not be content to have the old lady rise stiffly to her feet and hobble into the kitchen? He explains that the Materns had an instinct for operatic behavior; but, in fact, the scene is a warning that the author refuses to attempt a rational explanation of human behavior.

The following section, which deals with Amsel's ancestry, shows how justified this irrationalism is. His father kept a general store in the fishing village of Schiewenhorst—a fact which invites Grass to deploy his skill in the matter of invoking sights and smells. However, the father's business acumen raises the apparently absurd, yet actually vital, question as to whether he was a Jew as the villagers were inclined to suspect. From early childhood, Eddi Amsel is involved in this web of undefined, irrational hostility that finds expression in a grotesque incident at his christening. The party sets out, soberly enough, for the church, until a cloud of five hundred birds casts its shadow over the procession and sends the guests scuttling for safety. Thus singled out, Eddi develops, in self-defense, a skill in making scarecrows which sets him apart from his fellow men: "He had no objection to birds: but the birds . . . objected to him and his scarecrow-making" (p. 32).

The "Tenth Shift" in Brauxel's mine is devoted to the problem of what constitutes Jewishness, the strange ailment that afflicts Amsel. Unlike Adler (=eagle), which is immediately recognizable as Jewish, Amsel is surely a Dutch name. On the other hand, the death-bed confession of Amsel's mother reveals her husband's descent from a family of Pomeranian Jewish tailors. Books on the elusive subject seem to have an unpredictable effect that compounds the confusion. There is, for instance, Otto Weininger's *Sex and Character,* popular at the turn of the century, which attributes female characteristics to the Jewish race and denies the Jews a soul. Improbably enough, it was this book that inspired Amsel's father in a vain attempt to overcome his Jewishness by founding the local Sports Club and dying for his country at Verdun.

Brauxel has preserved and still consults Amsel's copy of Weininger's work. Later, when Brauxel and Amsel are revealed as one and the same person, the reader realizes that Weininger's strange theories about soulless beings are parodied in the scarecrows. In a sense, then, Amsel's life, like that of his father, has been influenced by Weininger.

Certainly, the irrational powers of anti-Semitism are not to be underrated. Long before his mother's revelation of the family origins, Eddi Amsel's schoolmates taunt him as "Itzig"—a contemptuous name for a Jew. Eddi's skill as a maker of scarecrows, however, earns him the grudging respect of Matern. When Eddi sells three scarecrows to a local farmer, Matern contemptuously terms their haggling over the price "Geschachere"—a word of Hebrew origin used to denote shifty dealing.

Further aspects of these scarecrows are revealed in fragmentary form at the beginning of each section or "Shift" where Brauxel gives his readers glimpses into the operation of his mine. He gradually discloses the fact that the mine produces scarecrows, the design of which is based on Amsel's naïve diary entries (with a Joycean delight in parody, Grass composes these in art critics' jargon). Brauxel sells these scarecrows, for he reports sending cards to his business associates (mention of the death of the Socialist Hinrich Kopf shows that it is New Year, 1962).

Other hints, especially at the beginning of the "Fourteenth Shift," where Brauxel speaks of his co-authors, also suggests that the mining in which he is engaged signifies the production of his chronicle—the common figure of the author delving into his subconscious. It gradually dawns on the reader that Brauxel and his fellow authors are engaged in writing the three parts of *Hundejahre*. Mysterious hints are dropped, the meaning of which becomes clear only at a later stage of the narrative. Thus we read that a newspaper article on Amsel's scarecrows appeared "before the world has registered either Harry Liebenau or his cousin Tulla." The reader eventually discovers that Harry is the author of the second of the three books that constitute *Hundejahre,* and that his contribution takes the form of love letters addressed to his cousin Tulla. Tulla has already been foreshadowed as a historical figure, the daughter of Kynstute of Swantopolk who haunts the marshes of the Vistula landscape. Thus Brauxel and his authors are substitutes for Grass himself who is clearly lurking behind their activities: "Brauxel and his fellow authors had learned their trade with someone who, during his lifetime, worked hard on lacquered tin" (p. 117).

The authors are continually urged to study Amsel's diaries, so that a connection is established between the scarecrows and the book produced in Brauxel's mine. This association helps to identify the scarecrows as ciphers of man's creative activities. The scarecrows, however, which make Brauxel a wealthy man and keep Amsel's persecutors at bay, also threaten their creators. Amsel has a bird's name, and Brauxel at this stage of his chronicle pointedly refers to himself as "der Federführende," which means not only "the wielder of a pen," but also "one who wears feathers."

In his rambling quest for the underlying significance of the narrative, Brauxel pauses to discuss aesthetic theory. In the "Fourteenth Shift" he mentions the "new French school," presumably that of Robbe-Grillet and *le nouveau roman*—and adduces a theory from Amsel's diary: "Models should preferably be taken from Nature." This thesis is immediately nullified, however, by the corollary: "Everything that can be stuffed is part of Nature, for instance, dolls" (p. 52). Abandoning theory, Brauxell turns to his real subject, Danzig.

The first approach, factual and impersonal, reproduces extracts from thirteenth-century documents. The other method, used immediately afterwards, employs childhood memories and folklore. Amsel and Matern go out into the damp cow pastures at dawn to observe the eels which, in accordance with a once widespread folk belief, crawl through the grass to suck milk from cows. Brauxel tacitly concludes that history and legend are inseparable and equally valid modes. In sections nineteen and twenty, Amsel's recurring vision of the twelve headless nuns and knights extends through European history from the period of the Teutonic Knights (Ragnit in East Prussia, the stronghold of the Order from 1397 to 1409 is mentioned) to the First World War and the Second Battle of Tannenberg in 1914.

The historical vision ends abruptly when a fanatical Mennonite burns down Matern's mill. This happens on Candlemass Day (February 2) which, as the reader learns later, is roughly the date of the end of the world, according to astrologists' predictions. The narrative passes, without transition, to the everyday world in which Amsel and Matern travel daily to school by the Werder Light Railway. For the time being, Amsel is in the ascendancy, and Matern is content to act as his porter and general assistant. However, the impermanence of this situation is hinted at when the boys change clothes. The narrative soon slides back into a grotesque subterranean region.

The two boys discover a secret passage leading from the school, by way of a sewer, to the banks of the Radaune River, with a view across Danzig. Exploring farther, they find a lateral passage leading under the medieval Trinity Church. It is in this suggestive position that they find a skeleton, whereupon Matern starts to beat Amsel, uttering the insulting "Itzich" in recollection of Golgotha, the place of skulls. The overpowering impulse to persecute is associated not only with the dark foundations of the Christian church, where the scene takes place, but also with Matern's genealogy (he broods on his Slav ancestor, the bandit Materna), with history in general (Amsel finds a soldier's button from the Napoleonic Wars near the skeleton), and with the stars (the prediction of the end of the world crops up here again). The passage under the church points ahead to Brauxel's mine, depicted at the end of the novel, as a kind of collective unconscious where history lurks.

The same spirit of doom inherent in this passage prevails even in the streets of Danzig. It is concentrated especially in a taxidermist's shop which displays, among other things, an eagle pouncing on a lamb. Under the influence of these events, Amsel builds a huge bird that terrifies the villagers to such an extent that they insist he remove his workshop. He burns his rags and other material, while an occasional cry of "Itzich" is heard. Plainly, however, the "Great Dicky-bird"—a bird in the shape of a scarecrow which embodies both victim and persecutor—will rise, like Phoenix, from the ashes. After every catastrophe or recurring end of the world, human affairs may be expected to resume their absurd course. In fact, far from being shy of symbolism (and belying Grass' hearty assurances that he is a mere storyteller), Brauxel announces his intention of constructing a similar Phoenix in Western Germany.

The usual abrupt change to sober reality sends Amsel and Matern to boarding-school in the city of Danzig—the *Conradinum* of *Katz und Maus*. The traditional skill with which Grass reproduces the Principal's ready flow of conversation with the boys' parents, or the scenes in the school playground patrolled by Oswald Brunies (also encountered in *Katz und Maus*) emphasize his refusal to be confined to one mode of observation.

Matern and Amsel, who are so different in temperament, confirm the validity of their temperaments by means of different repulsive acts. Walter practices "Schlagball" (a form of rounders once popular in Northern Germany) by hitting at hopping frogs with his bats, while Amsel, who loathes the game, feigns sickness and, at the same time, proves his courage by swallowing the cast-off tails of newts with something of Mahlke's powers of endurance.

When the school is transferred for fourteen days to summer quarters in the Saskochin Forest, the grotesque resumes its sway. The panorama is enriched by the vocabulary of gypsies and the names of the primitive spirit that haunt the German-Polish forest: "Da krümmt sich Beng, Balderle fliegt auf, Schlaflichter wehen, Oichterles wandern, Bäume belaxeln sich, Mängische wechseln" (p. 122). Grass explains the principle applied here: "Brauxel, who wields the pen, suffers from the inability to describe a landscape devoid of people" (p. 113). Where Adalbert Stifter was content with the blue hills of the Bohemian Forests, Brauxel, alias Grass, must place figures in his landscape. Inanimate nature is meaningless divorced from human activity. Grass has already characterized the barren soil of the region through a gesture of the peasants: they are always stooping under their umbrellas to pick up stones and throw them onto the neighbor's field. The forest is embodied in a strange gypsy, Bildandengero (= the toothless), lurking in the thickets with his child.

Matern establishes contact with the gypsy while retrieving a ball from the undergrowth where Bildandengero is crouching. Finally, Matern and Amsel arrive in time to witness a strange scene in an abandoned distillery in the forest, possibly on the Polish side of the former border. Bildandengero and his company of "Gakkos" (also called "Ziganken," "Mängische," "Ballertmeger" or "Forest Hussars") take advantage of Brunies' habit of surreptitiously cooking toffee in the forest to leave him with the weeping bundle they had carried with them and which turns out to be a six-month-old girl.

We have now reached the year 1927, the year in which Tulla, representing the spirit of the times, is born. She becomes the persecutor of Brunies—whose sweet tooth brings about his downfall—and his equally harmless adopted daughter Jenny. Much in the manner of Alfred Döblin's novel, *Berlin-Alexanderplatz,* the private event of Tulla's birth is heralded by a series of public events that suggest the imperceptible transition from one to the other, and the strange and secret associations between them.

In Döblin's novel, such events as a strike in Oslo, a bicycle race in Stuttgart, and unrest in the Saar are reported as a parallel to the hero's activities on a certain day in 1928.[3] Some of the events that take place on June 11, 1927 (the day of Tulla's birth) are trivial enough (for instance, a concert given by the police band in the *Kurgarten* at Zoppot), but others are suggestive of the future, such as the Nazis announcing mass meetings to discuss "A People in

Distress: Who Will Come to Its Aid?" A certain Dr. Citron still has his practice in Langfuhr; this apparently dull fact acquires significance in the concluding half of the sentence: "later he had to flee to Sweden." Next to the report about the Jewish doctor is an announcement of the appearance of Heidegger's *Sein und Zeit* (Time and Being), anticipating the end of the Second Book, when the final messages from Hitler's Berlin bunker parody the philosopher's style. Even the broader context of the weather and the stars may be relevant. Tulla's birthday places her, in the astrological terms prevalent in this book, under the influence of Gemini and makes her as changeable as the weather on this day.

Tulla is a product of her time and place. The account that Harry Liebenau gives of her in the "Love Letters" which constitute the Second Book is no more hostile and indignant than Oskar's account of the Nazi era; for Harry is in love with Tulla. Reason and intellect are of no help to him. His love is not based on illusions, for he clearly perceives that she is cruel and unclean in her habits. Harry, plainly a trained observer of considerable intelligence, submits to a searching cross-examination by Brauxel before he is allowed to begin. He passes his test with flying colors because he knows not only the names of the streets of the old town, but also such facts as the date of the introduction of the rubber truncheon and the fate of the last chairman of the Liberal Party who had spent some time in the local concentration camp. Whether such facts are important or trivial, no one can really say. In his passion for the truth, Harry includes everything.

The Love Letters of Harry Liebenau

The first letters concern Tulla Pokriefke's ancestry. She is not only a child of her era, but her roots go deep into the region. The origins of her mother's family are lost in a tangle of Polish and German names, while her father's family has lived for generations in a district called the *Koschneiderei* on whose vanished dialect Grass lingers. Tulla's close associations with the region are emphasized. At the age of seven she suffered from the lack of calcium characteristic of this province's soil. The name Tulla (her real name was Ursula) corresponds to that of a water sprite which made its home in the local lake of Osterwick, called, in Polish, "Ostrow" and, in the local dialect, "Oustrewitsch."

The beginning of the end of this tradition is indicated when the family moves to Danzig to join the urban proletariat. Harry Liebenau's mother, *née* Pokriefke, persuades her husband to give her brother a job in his carpenter's workshop. Tulla's father is a clumsy worker, capable of performing only the simplest tasks. He boils the glue, with the result that the Pokriefke apartment as well as Tulla smell of bones. This theme is later developed into a cipher for the pungent cruelty of Tulla's character and even brought into association with Stutthof, the concentration camp near Danzig. For the present, however, the reader is told merely that the sight of Tulla terrified Brunies' adopted daughter Jenny. In her very real person, Tulla sums up the lean soil and the bloody history of the East German border region.

An excursion into the future establishes Tulla's association with the history of her era. The *Koschneiderei*, Polish after the Treaty of Versailles, is incorporated into the German Reich after the invasion of Poland in 1939. Grass sums up these historical events by his customary method of laconic apocope and the running together of clichés. Thus "Abheutefrühvieruhrfünfundvierzig" is a weary reference to Hitler's speech to the Reichstag on September 1, 1939: "Since 5:45 A.M. we have been returning fire, and from now on bombs will be met with bombs."

The Liebenaus' watchdog, Harras, throws another indirect light on history at this point. His essentially German nature is emphasized: "No longhaired Belgian Groenendael, but a wirehaired German shepherd" (p. 147). In the beginning he is strong, healthy, handsome, and rough, but not really brutal; but his character is to show a steady deterioration in subsequent years. For the length of a dog's life, Harras leaves his traces all over Danzig. The places he visits are significant: the linden trees in the Hindenburgallee where, as we have learned in *Die Blechtrommel*, deserters are hanged as the Russians are advancing; the flag poles in front of the Sports Palace where the Nazis hold their mass meetings, and the lamp posts of Langfuhr, soon to be blacked out in the war. Grass joins in the solemn game of literary interpretation by pointing out that the number on the dog's license adds up to thirteen.

In such an apparently inconsequential, but actually calculated fashion, Harry's epistolary narrative reaches the year 1932. The mood is sober. Matern and Amsel are, for the time being, no longer the legendary figures of the First Book but simply two small boys helping Brunies to push his plump foster-daughter along the promenade at Brösen in an old-fashioned perambulator. The story of her gypsy descent has already been dismissed as "a typical Papa Brunies story."

Other grotesque incidents receive a summary treatment: Oskar, encountered on the walk, is introduced simply as the grocer's son "not quite right in the head" beating his drum in time to the singing of a group of *Jungvolk;* Tulla has to confine her persecution to the act of spitting into Jenny's empty pram. By next summer—the year in which Hitler becomes Chancellor—Jenny is not so closely guarded, and Tulla takes the opportunity to bully her more actively. She tries to force her to eat a jellyfish and seeks to make her fear Harras who seems to enjoy the game and is reluctant to come away when Harry calls him off. According to the principle implicit in all of Grass' novels, the persecutor must also play the role of victim, and this she does when her deaf-mute brother Konrad, whom she dearly loves, is drowned.

The incident of Tulla's mourning was published separately in an anthology of modern German prose in 1962.[4] It was presumably part of the novel *Kartoffelschalen* (Potato Peelings) which Grass later abandoned. It begins with Harry's father taking Harras to the Danzig police barracks for stud purposes. While they are waiting in the lieutenant's office, they have time to admire the pictures of prize-winning dogs on the wall, topped by a signed photograph of President Hindenburg. The connection between Harras and German history thus established, the lieutenant warns Harry's father, pocketing the stud fee, that the dog shows signs of reverting to type: "The pedigree clearly shows that, three generations back, the animal came from Lithuania. There could be a mutation suddenly, any day now. It wouldn't be the first time" (p. 166). The anthology version is even more explicit on the impending danger because here the lieutenant mentions the possibility of "the wolf breaking through." Grass may have found the parallel with German history after 1933 too obvious, too "symbolical," and chose to omit it from the later version. In *Hundejahre* the police officer hints that the dog has been wrongly trained by Harry.

But, as Harry goes on to demonstrate in his chronicle, it was Tulla who was responsible for Harras' deterioration. She mourned for her brother by crouching in Harras' kennel for seven days and nights, sharing the dog's bowl of offal, the appearance and origin of which Grass describes in minute detail. It is the same stew of heart, kidneys, and lights with which the cat does penance in the poem, although Grass here enlarges on its jellylike consistency, the gristle at the bottom of the bowl, and the surface of congealed fat. Even the master himself, Harry's father, cannot control Harras. When he tries to intervene, the dog knocks him to the ground, whereupon Liebenau finds a pretext, some half-hour later, to beat the apprentice (an unfortunate youth who later loses two fingers in the circular saw). Later the reader can observe the principle at work behind this semi-comic interlude. Jenny has to pay for Tulla's suffering as the apprentice did for his master's humiliation; and childish retaliation is raised to a law of human existence.

Harras has been allowed to tyrannize the carpenter's yard— enough to ruin the effects of the most careful training. The subsequent events place this deterioration against a background which explains the dog's role as a cipher of German history. One of the puppies resulting from Harras' union with the bitch Thekla at the police barracks is presented to Hitler as a gift from the city of Danzig on his forty-sixth birthday (April 20, 1935). Harry Liebenau's subsequent class report on this event is a model of deflating mockery that places the phenomenon Hitler in a world of childish illusion. Although well acquainted with the realities of dog breeding, Harry feels obliged to prattle harmlessly about mother, father, and children. The teacher, Miss Spollenhauer (familiar, to readers of *Die Blechtrommel* as Oskar's teacher for one day) contrives the following exemplary dialogue with Harry:

"Why did the *Gauleiter* give the little dog Prinz to our *Führer?*"

"Because it was the *Führer's* birthday, and he has always wanted a little dog from our city."

"And why does the little dog Prinz enjoy it so much on the Obersalzberg that he doesn't want to go back to his mummy any more?"

"Because our *Führer* loves dogs and is always kind to dogs."

"And why should we be glad that the little dog Prinz is with the *Führer?*" (p. 182)

Wolfishness and servility, amply displayed in this canine dialogue, make the dog an appropriate cipher for the Hitler era. This is shown in an episode in which Hitler relinquishes his place to a dog. As the owner of Harras, Harry's father is invited—summoned, rather—to visit the *Führer*, who is in Danzig for the opening of the Polish campaign. Hitler is unable to receive his visitors, but, in compensation, Harry and his father are allowed to see Prinz, accompanied by an SS man, lounging elegantly in the winter garden of Hitler's hotel. Liebenau later announces importantly to bystanders: "No, well, not the *Führer*, we didn't see him, but we did see his dog. Black he is, I tell you, as black as our Harras was" (p. 305). Nazi racial theory, too, is reduced to the animal level. Rauschning (a leader of the Danzig Senate who records in his memoirs the presentation of a dog to Hitler on his forty-sixth birthday by Gauleiter Forster of Danzig) is accused of describing Prinz as a wolfhound, a mistake parrotted Harry complains, by all subsequent historians. Harry's father shows another expert, who is not satisfied with Harras' pedigree, off the premises.

The narrator's attention now shifts to the victims of the new order. They meet at the house of the piano teacher Felsner-Imbs, Grass' accomplished portrait of a provincial Wagnerian. His most gifted pupils are Eddi Amsel and Jenny Brunies, both of them plump and musical. Eddi, however, is not so helpless as his appearance suggests. His artistic gifts have given him entrée to the local brothel. Plainly a man of parts, he obtains permission to draw Harras (whom he renames Pluto) and, to Tulla's annoyance, gains complete control over the dog: "And now, would you be so good as to turn your noble head a little to the left; so, so, that's it, Pluto, hold it" (p. 193). He deals easily with August Pokriefke's clumsily sarcastic inquiries about his political allegiance, so that it looks for a time as if the accomplished, sensitive artist were master over the forces of barbarism. This is not so, however, since his self-possession is not proof against the cry of "Itzig" which Tulla sets up on his next visit to Liebenau's lumberyard. The cry, monotonously repeated, echoes around the yard, drowning even the saw, so that people come to their windows. Even Matern finds himself strangely helpless, although his aspect is threatening enough to prevent August Pokriefke from spitting.

Hounded out of the yard by Tulla and forbidden to return, Eddi takes up sports and, on the death of his mother, invests his inherited capital in Switzerland. Encouraged by Eddi's example, Jenny takes ballet lessons, even though she is pink and fat. The pattern of the Second Book is thus established. The victims are cast down by persecution, only to emerge again with improved skills and abilities—a process which is shortly to take on grotesque forms. Related, concurrent themes are Harry's hopeless love for Tulla and Walter Matern's moody, wavering uncertainty, both calculated to ensure that the reader is deprived of the easy expedient of attributing all the virtues to a plainly identifiable victim.

Tulla's persecution of the pretentious Felsner-Imbs is as amusing as the exploits of Max and Moritz. When he enters the carpenter's yard to beg for brief silence while he practices "something complicated, a so-called adagio," Tulla unchains Harras who playfully tears the frightened musician's flapping frock-coat. The whole incident is introduced by Harry's ardent protestation of love for Tulla: "The woodshed belonged to you. All the gluepots and fine curly wood-shavings belonged to you. I write for you, even if I write for Brauxel" (p. 212).

Eddi is farsighted enough to take the matter seriously and to acquire the musician's frock-coat as material for the construction of the first scarecrow. Harry's chronicle, hitherto sober enough, now makes the inevitable slide into the grotesque. Thus Eddi's motive for making scarecrows is given as his desire "to prove his productivity against a dangerously productive outside world." He moves into a villa in a select part of Danzig, renting two rooms to Matern who is learning to be an actor by playing small parts in the *Stadttheater*. With his sensitive organ for the shape of future events, Amsel starts to work on figures of Stormtroopers. To further his investigation, he persuades Walter to join the local SA unit. With this act, Amsel seals his own fate. Walter finds many former Communists among the Troopers, for, as the chief Sawatski explains with brutal humor, the *Führer* rejoices more over one converted Communist than over ten cautious former Liberals.

The second assault on Felsner-Imbs is less comic than the first. This time Harras needs no urging, nor is he at all playful. On the other hand, the musician ably defends himself with his umbrella, although he cannot prevent Jenny from being thrown into the gutter. As before, Harras and Tulla escape unscathed while Harry is punished by Liebenau. Tulla is seen soon afterwards as the presiding genius of a "Saalschlacht" of a type common during the 1930's, a political meeting followed by a beerhouse brawl, all of which Grass renders in a chopped rhythm punctuated by the howl, "Ei wei, schalle machei!" The incident provides the observant Eddi with inspiration for his most ambitious work to date, representing Schiller and Goethe, together with Horst Wessel and other martyrs of the Nazi movement, dressed in the brown uniforms of Stormtroopers. Included in the group is a figure which grinds its teeth in imitation of Walter Matern.

The group of scarecrows illustrates the pessimistic attitude toward progress in human affairs adumbrated throughout Grass' novels. The recurring futility of history is suggested in the pairs of place names (Hindenburgallee/Clay-Allee) that link prewar Danzig and postwar Berlin. The third attack on Felsner-Imbs is not at all comic because this time Harras makes sure of his prey and sends him to the hospital with a lacerated thigh. The other persecutions are grotesque. Tulla makes Jenny dance in the snow before the Gutenberg memorial, where an evil spirit called "Kumpätsch" is said to live, until she falls down exhausted. Finally, the long-awaited persecution of Amsel takes place when nine masked men, one of them certainly Matern, attack him and leave him, too, lying in the snow. The thirty-two teeth he loses provide another disturbing motif.

The scenes and episodes at this point of the story are calculated to provide a number of ciphers that will reflect the Nazi era. The repeated summary of Harras' "points" in dog-breeders' jargon underlines the combination of bestiality with sober matter-of-factness and technical expertise characteristic of the era. But there is also a strong fairy-tale element in the narrative (Kumpätsch for instance) which suggests that the malignancy of the period is atavistic and ineradicable. Not to be neglected is the strong comic element present, for example, in the attacks on Felsner-Imbs; for the Nazi era was undoubtedly, from some points of view, a lengthy slapstick farce.

At this point the story might well have ended; actually, however, it is not yet halfway completed. The two victims are somewhat perfunctorily resurrected: Amsel as Haseloff, a kind of Wandering Jew; Jenny as "the new Jenny." In accordance with Grass' belief in the value of "asceticism," both emerge remote and refined by suffering.

No abrupt return to sober reality follows. For a time the narrative lingers on the theme of ballet, an art in which, for Grass, the grotesque mingles imperceptibly with the real. Every day the new Jenny goes to ballet classes in the company of Tulla who refuses to be shaken off. The story marks time at this point while the narrator plays with the technical terms of ballet or dwells on the exact route taken by Jenny and Tulla. This deliberate monotony creates a sense of brooding danger which reflects the historical situation—the pause before Hitler attacked Poland in 1939—on the plane of petty, everyday existence.

The other persecutor, Matern, is also biding his time, though without Tulla's singlemindedness. He obtains casual work as an actor and is expelled from the SA for stealing unit funds, although his *Sturmführer* declares that Matern will never be banished from his heart. The theft is, we may assume, a devious outlet for Matern's shame and discontent with himself. After a period of drunken musing on the banks of the Vistula and several visits to the Liebenau lumberyard, Matern poisons Harras, the "Catholic Nazi swine." As an anti-

Nazi, he is beaten up, not too severely, by the police in Düsseldorf. Feeling in a vague way that he has done his duty for the anti-Fascist cause and presumably satisfied with his self-imposed penance, he finally joins the German Army in time for Hitler's Polish campaign.

The whole affair takes place with an inevitability, as if everybody concerned were playing an assigned part in a plot already known. Nobody is shocked or surprised that Matern should kill Harras, for there is tacit agreement that the dog is a Nazi, just as everybody agrees that Amsel is a Jew.

Tulla, too, comes to play her part when her period of waiting ends, a point which coincides with the outbreak of the equally inevitable Second World War. Her persecution of Jenny, like that of Felsner-Imbs, takes the form of three ordeals, traditional to the fairy tale. The incident is introduced by Harry's attempt to guess the name of Jenny's new ballet-master much like the Princess trying to guess the name of Rumpelstilskin. "Is he called, perhaps, Steppuhn, Steppoleit or Stephanowski?" (p. 307). The first stage of the persecution is reached when Tulla places nine leeches on Jenny; the second occurs when she locks her, together with Harry, into a brewery icehouse.

In the third and climactic stage of the persecution, Tulla reports Jenny's foster-father, Brunies, to the authorities for eating the sweet vitamin tablets provided as a supplement for children's diet from 1941 onwards. Brunies disappears into the concentration camp of Stutthof, established in 1939 at an ancient German settlement near Danzig. Grass' narrative, which consistently refuses to distinguish between the real and the unreal, provides the equivalent for this grotesque institution which he never describes in detail, although it is always present in the background.

Haseloff rescues Jenny and Felsner-Imbs by taking them to Paris, from where Jenny regularly writes to Harry, reporting her progress in Haseloff's ballet school. Harry is left to the bleakness of wartime Danzig and to its equivalent, Tulla, who is ugly, with a pale, pimply face and is, moreover, promiscuous. Yet Harry's love for Tulla, like Grass' love for Danzig, persists in spite of his clear perception of her ugliness and cruelty.

The end of Danzig and of Harry's narrative is approaching. The epistolary pretense is dropped, so that the letters no longer begin "Dear Tulla" but "Once upon a time . . ."—a phrase which suggests the remote past: "Once upon a time there was a girl named Tulla," and "Once upon a time there was a city."

As the war closes in on Germany, Harry and his friends become

[113]

"Gymnasiasten in Uniform" and Harry serves as an anti-aircraft gunner. The unspoken threat of final catastrophe finds expression, in a devious way, by means of parodies of Heidegger's enigmatic style, which are to reach a climax with the fall of Berlin. The initiator of these parodies is Matern, who has returned from the Russian front, wounded and in a mood of brooding uncertainty. He finds eager pupils among his schoolboy subordinates. The joke, thin at first, gains in weight when the young soldiers and Matern move from the salubrious sandy coast to an artillery unit in the industrial dockside district of Kaiserhafen. The battery position is overrun with rats, and hunts are organized to the accompaniment of Heidegger, while the "ontical" voices of passing ships are heard. Thus, while Private Störtebeker is groping for rats in the camp sewer, he dignifies his simple occupation with this soliloquy:

The rat withdraws itself by de-concealing itself into the ratty. Thus the rat errates, illuminating it, the ratty with errancy. For the ratty has come-to-pass into the errancy in which it circumerrates the rat, thus giving-rise-to-error. Error is the essence of history. (p. 471)

While Störtebeker is disguising squalid actions under a cloak of pedantry, Grass is suggesting a parallel with Heidegger who was, for a time at least, a Nazi sympathizer who, in 1933, called upon Freiburg students to be loyal to *Volk* and *Führer*. The incursion of convoluted Heideggerian metaphysics is also intended to demonstrate the decay of German language and morals (similar to the parodies of Weininger and Benn).

How far this decay has progressed is revealed when the cause of the rats' presence is discussed: a mountain of bones which spreads a stench over the whole area. At night, when the guns are firing, the pile is added to; but everyone resolutely ignores it—everyone, that is, except Tulla who one day jerks a casual thumb and remarks, "That's a heap of bones." Harry and the others vaguely contradict, but Tulla insists: "I bet those are bones. What's more, they're *human* bones, so there!" (p. 370). Störtebeker tries to evade the issue with a snatch of pseudo-Heidegger, but she crosses a barbed-wire fence and brings back a human skull as evidence. Her only reward for her frankness is a blow from Matern.

Harry Liebenau has seen Prinz, the dog sired by Harras, at the opening of Hitler's Polish campaign. Now, when the great retreat begins, he sees the dog again in a newsreel of Hitler's East Prussian headquarters (where, as a matter of historical fact, Hitler kept a bitch called Blondi, given to him by Bormann as consolation for the disaster at Stalingrad). The slide into the abyss is displayed under many aspects, public and private. Tulla, representing her time and place so accurately, suffers a miscarriage in a bleak winter field. On the plane of actual historical events, Stauffenberg's unsuccessful attempt on Hitler's life is treated with the irony that Hitler always arouses in Grass: "The record with the Twilight of the Gods lay ready." A bomb cripples Jenny while she is rehearsing Haseloff's new scarecrow ballet. Even Harry Liebenau's stolid father is affected. Apparently unmoved, he has watched his trade deteriorate, and Brunies disappear into Stutthof. Now the accumulated fury breaks out; he seizes an ax and destroys Harras' kennel.

Finally, Harry, the chronicler, departs for the front, as Grass himself did in 1945—just in time to take part in the closing stages of the German defeat. He contrives to leave Danzig for the last time on the Number Five Tram on which Tulla is a conductress. Unaffected by his departure, cruel, indifferent, and unmistakably proletarian, she represents the Danzig that Harry glimpses through a hole scratched in the blacked-out window. Harry succeeds in casting off his obsession with Tulla only when, in the course of the headlong retreat, a German tank backs into a glass blower's storage shed. This noisy destruction of a traditional craft, indissolubly associated with Silesia through Gerhart Hauptmann, seems to convince Harry that Eastern Germany is lost. At any rate, Tulla ceases to haunt him, while the remainder of his letters contain no further reminiscences of Danzig and the Vistula.

Harry's chronicle concludes with the fall of Berlin. The last act of the Third Reich, dramatized in numerous reports, is turned to ridicule. Once more the dog Prinz replaces his owner as the center of attention by escaping on April 20, 1945—Hitler's fifty-sixth birthday—from the oppressive atmosphere of the bunker underneath the Chancellery. Now all the remaining groups and fragments of armies receive instructions to recapture the runaway in a style that simultaneously parodies Nazi propaganda, military communications, and Heidegger's language. These efforts are an equivalent of Hitler's absurd preoccupation with the unreal question of his succession.

Prinz, whose thoughts are reported in Grass' most extensive use of interior monologue, explains his reasons for escaping, at first in farcical Heideggerian terminology: "Because no stable dog-here, dog-there, dog-now . . . Because always Being-Locked-in-Room"

(p. 423). More concretely, he complains about the years he has been on the move and proceeds to list some of Hitler's operational plans, from "Case White" against Poland to "Barbarossa" against Russia. Political satire enters the picture in the efforts made by the Allies to capture the ex-Fascist German dog for themselves, in the rumors that he is in the Vatican, and finally in his rejection of Eastern Germany for the West.

Matern's Chronicle

The dog provides a link with the next section, the "Materniaden," with its lengthy attacks on West German public figures. Matern's wanderings start with his release from a British prisoner-of-war camp where Mr. Brook(e)s, a metamorphosis of the ubiquitous Brauxel elicits from him protests of anti-Fascist sentiment that, although not entirely fabricated, inevitably ring false. The falsity of his anti-Fascist pose and the futility of his efforts to punish former Nazis and to avenge their misdeeds is to be the burden of the following "Materniaden." The situation is emphasized in the opening sentence: "The dog stands central." Even before his release from the camp, Prinz is dogging Matern's footsteps. Wandering southwest through a ruined Germany, Matern decides to name his dog Pluto after a mine in the Ruhr district. They enter Pluto's kingdom by descending into the cellar of a ruined building. There appropriately, they find a pile of posters bearing Hitler's portrait. Matern's first act of de-Nazification is to attempt to tear them up, but the dog growls threateningly, and Matern desists.

The monotony and listlessness that have pervaded this part of the narrative yield to a new tone of hectic drama when Matern discovers his mission of revenge: "I come to judge with a black dog . . ." From the men's toilet in Cologne station, Matern sets out to rectify the world's evil. There, among the random scribblings and graffiti, he finds the names and addresses of former Nazis. Cologne has been chosen possibly out of deference to Heinrich Böll in whose stories this station is the starting point for a new life after the War.

Matern's first avenging visit is to Sawatski, his former superior officer in the SA. He finds Sawatski comfortably installed near Cologne with a wife from the Rhineland. Matern's intention already loses some of its righteous purity when Sawatski points out that he, Matern, was one of the nine men (not eight!) who attacked Amsel. The whole action ends with the three of them, fuddled, in one bed. Undeterred, Matern leaves hastily and continues to pose as God's scourge. Every attempt fails. The former captain of Matern's AA battery, celebrating Christmas in the bosom of his family, wittily points out Matern's resemblance to Beckmann in Borchert's *Draussen vor der Tür* ("an excellent piece of theater . . . Weren't you an actor by profession?"). When he meets his former bullying drill-instructor, whose wife has been killed in an air-raid, Matern is reduced to killing the man's pet canary. In Göttingen he throws a former Nazi judge's stamp-collection, followed by tweezers and stamp-hinges, into the stove, while the aged father mutters about "vandals." He visits Heidegger's house and rattles at the gate, shouting insults.

Matern's mission ends with his infecting the wives and daughters of his victims with gonorrhea which he contracted in Saarbrücken. This gives Grass a chance to assemble a list of dialect words for this disease which correspond to the districts that Matern visits all over the four Occupation Zones. The episode is far too long, like much in the last book, but it serves the purpose of demonstrating how revenge blurs still further the uncertain boundaries between guilt and innocence. The reader can sympathize with a former Nazi youth leader, turned liberal, who exclaims, "We wanted to go Eastwards with Hölderlin and Heidegger in our knapsacks. And now we sit here in the West with the pox" (p. 471).

Wearied by erotic exertions and self-disgust, Matern makes a last, vain attempt to arouse the conscience of the Church. The attempt falls, with Grass' usual literary interpretation of figures of speech, on deaf ears. The ear in question belongs to a priest who formerly supported the Nazis and the SA. From the penitent's side of a confession box, Matern tries to thrust a knitting needle into the priest's ear, but the confessor feels nothing and blandly repeats the formula, "Ego te absolvo . . ." In fact, the only sufferer from Matern's rage with the Church is Inge Sawatski whom he brutally mishandles after she has left her husband to follow him.

Having shown the futility of revenge, the chronicle now turns aside to attack, at great length, the postwar "Economic Miracle." The attack, a strange mixture of polemic indignation and farce, has a grotesque starting point in the mealworms, which Matern's father rescues with great difficulty from flour brought from the Danzig windmill. "Goldmouth," alias Haseloff, who is very active in the days after the 1949 currency reform, sets him up, with his worms, in a windmill near the Dutch border as an adviser to the newly emerging tycoons. Grass reviews the leading figures in postwar Western Germany who consult the prophetic worms speaking through the miller.

Axel Springer thus receives the inspiration to found his newspaper empire when the worms prophecy the day when "three million illiterate readers will breakfast daily with the *Bild*." The Roman Catholic Church, too, is represented in close union with the Christian Democrat Party encouraging separate schools for Catholics and Protestants and discouraging the reunification of East and West Germany. Ludwig Erhard, allowed to swallow a worm, becomes the prophet of the new prosperity, while the Socialists can attribute their lack of success to their failure to consult the worms. They dismiss the whole affair as "medieval superstition" (p. 501).

The whole episode is based on a play of words, a literal rendering of the idiom "da ist ein Wurm drin" (there is a worm in it) applied to suspicious or dubious situations. The German revival, Grass implies, is not a genuinely fresh start but is corrupt at the outset and rooted in the peasant cunning and superstition of the past. In Böll's novel *Billiard um halbzehn* Hindenburg is the villain from the past who still infects the present. A portrait of Hindenburg hangs in Matern's mill. Grass makes the interesting suggestion that corruption is necessary to government when the disappearance of the miller and the theft of a sack with worms is attributed to East German agents who, by resorting to the sources of power, can crush the Berlin uprising of 1953 and thus confirm Ulbricht in office.

This line of thought, however, is not developed. Walter Matern, who has assisted his father in the days of the mill's prosperity, now resumes his wanderings with his aging dog. He visits the Sawatskis, who are prospering in Düsseldorf, the capital of Germany's wealthiest *Land*, for which Grass finds half a page of insulting epithets. In *Die Blechtrommel*, Düsseldorf was characterized by the *Zwiebelkeller*, where guests rid themselves of inhibitions with the help of raw onions. Now, in the later stages of Germany's prosperity, this naïve institution is replaced by the "Morgue" (*Leichenhalle*) where the dominant figure is a partly dissected Swedish film star in a glass case. Surgical instruments serve as knife and fork and, most importantly, young doctors seated at the bar are prepared to chat about medical matters over a glass of champagne. Matern accompanies the Sawatskis to this restaurant. Yet even when the dessert is brought to him, artfully contrived in the shape of thirty-two teeth; the sight, which has in the past aroused him, presumably as a reminder of his guilt toward Amsel, now disgusts him. He tries to take up sports again, and Grass skillfully describes the decay of an aging sportsman. He turns to refereeing, insists on telling young players of his anti-

Fascist exertions, and finds himself expelled as a Communist just as he was once expelled from the Danzig Sports Club and the SA.

With his recurring life patterns, Matern is psychologically convincing as an individual; yet he also successfully represents the ideological listlessness and bewilderment of postwar Germany, where the recent past—to quote the historian Golo Mann—appeared "as if the whole affair had been a comedy in the style of the Captain of Köpenick, murderous like no other prank in world history, but a prank all the same, a mere swindle that nobody, now that it had been uncovered, was prepared to have had anything to do with." [5]

Matern's quest for guilty individuals has led to no satisfactory results, and an incident that occurs when he and Inge visit a fairground confirms him in his decision to abandon his vengeful mission. He catches a glimpse of a former police major who broke his ribs while interrogating him in Düsseldorf. Matern sets out in pursuit of the major, who is wearing the uniform of a rifle club, but when Matern and his dog, in true cinema style, plunge into the crowd to find the major, they see dozens of men wearing the same green uniform. The climax is reached when Matern bursts into a beer tent where no fewer than 132 men in green uniforms are posing for a group photograph.

By the ninety-first Materniad, the cry is "Call off your revenge, Matern!" (p. 546). However, Grass continues to add to his story as a sculptor might add a few more gargoyles to an already ornate façade. First there is the grotesque notion of "wonder spectacles" which allegedly reached the market in 1955. After some parodistic play with the distinction between *Erkennung* (identification) and *Erkenntnis* (cognition), the narrator reveals the brutal facts behind this abstract terminology. The spectacles enable young people under twenty-one to see those over thirty in their true light. The gift turns out to be of dubious value (as does a similar gift in Siegfried Lenz' short story, "Der Spielverderber"), so that the manufacturers, Brauxel & Co., withdraw the spectacles from circulation.

Matern sinks even lower. We now encounter him trying to poison the trees of Rolf Zander, a former Nazi fellow traveler turned theater critic whose style is characterized by a revolting insistence on "human" values. Zander surprises Matern at his nefarious operation, leads him into his comfortable living-room, and hires him for broadcasts of children's programs. This is Matern's final defeat; he who still has ambitions to play Schillerian roles becomes famous for his terrifying growls. The depth of humiliation is reached when Harry

Liebenau, now a highly literate and objectionable program organizer, engages Matern for the role of "Object under Discussion" in a new type of program.

The program takes the form of a grotesque radio interview with a background of rhymed commentary provided by a chorus of children. In the course of this discussion, Matern is baited by the "discussion leader" until he is brought to confess his participation in the persecution of Amsel. The themes and motifs of the novel are once more unravelled. The range is indicated in a childishly indecent verse about Jews on one hand, and, on the other, a nostalgic rhythmic passage, recited by Matern, on childhood in the Vistula region:

> Barfuss barfuss laufen die Kinder
> und finden Blaubeeren
> und suchen Bernstein.

("Barefoot, barefoot the children go and find bilberries and seek amber.")

The underlying theme is that of the novel as a whole: the impossibility of assigning guilt. Matern's defensive commonplaces are undoubtedly valid ("All men have something in common with Hitler"), but the discussion leader goads him on until he bursts out: "He got a thrashing, the Yid! Ei wai, schalle machai. Right in his ugly mug!" Yet Matern's last word is a sincere protest against anti-Fascist sentiment. The grotesque nature of the interview ensures that the exposure of Matern does nothing to establish any sense of cosmic order. It is both comic and demonic and recalls, in this, the mock trial in Dürrenmatt's *Die Panne* (The Breakdown) during which the four sedate bourgeois harass their victim until he confesses to a crime of which he was only partly aware.

The irrelevance of moral standards is clearly indicated in the fact that, to Matern, his birthday, which coincides with Hitler's, is as much a source of suppressed guilt as the assault on Amsel. The discussion leader has to wring from him the reluctant confession that he was born on April 20, under the sign of Aries. We are left to conclude that human actions are outside the province of the will and are governed, say, by the spirit inhabiting the Gutenberg memorial (which plays a role in the discussion) or perhaps by the stars. The idea is, of course, ridiculous, as is the whole discussion which derides the "avant-garde" and the high-pressure culture industry.

After his public humiliation, Matern decides to flee to Eastern Germany. Like most refugees, he has ideological reasons (the West is militaristic; the East is peace-loving), but also more personal and convincing ones (Inge is getting on his nerves). He leaves his dog behind and sets out on the interzonal train with the intention of making a fresh start. Needless to say, this is a journey made in vain, a fact emphasized by the conversation of the interzone travellers which blurs any distinction between "over here" and "over there." One grandmother even prattles indifferently about "here over there." During the old lady's endless monologue, Matern observes scarecrows in a variety of costumes and apparently running a relay race in pace with the train. The procession of ghosts does not stop when the train crosses the border into Eastern Germany, although the chronicler plays with the fancy that the scarecrows are enacting proletarian risings, especially the early sixteenth-century Peasants' Revolt. For all of Grass' assertions that he is a carefree story teller, bored by history, these scarecrows are heavy with historical significance ("botschaftenträchtig unterwegs"), with the weight of Germany's inescapable past. What is more, Hitler's black dog is following the train, apparently having broken loose from the Railway Mission (Lutheran Section) in Cologne station and with a new lease of youth.

Matern presumably realizes that flight is hopeless. At any rate, he gets out in West Berlin, ostensibly to buy supplies, and is met by Pluto and, close behind him, Goldmouth. While the trio wanders through a Berlin in which the real and the grotesque are inextricably entangled, Goldmouth relates once more the stories of Matern's persecution of his former self, Amsel. Matern reacts by failing to remember the past. Even when Goldmouth returns the knife that Matern threw into the Vistula in the opening scene, Mattern's memory is not jogged. Goldmouth thereupon takes Matern into a tavern, frequented by actors and managed by Jenny, a shrivelled, gray ghost of her former self. Finally he sets the whole place afire with the glowing cigarette ends which he carelessly casts over one shoulder. Amid the crackling of flames they exchange anecdotes, for, as Grass has said, "As long as we tell stories, we are still alive."

The fire, a strangely unreal blaze confined to Goldmouth's immediate vicinity and accompanied by snatches of the Catholic Mass that frighten away the Protestant firemen, suggests the conflagration of European history. Goldmouth, with his excessive cigarette consumption is, as it were, still smoking after the latest catastrophic blaze. Matern, however, stoutly refuses to think of recent history; he prefers to be reminded of earlier fires set by his Polish robber ancestors in the late fifteenth and early sixteenth centuries. Goldmouth continues to goad Matern with equivocal remarks on the

Germans: "Now, my dear Walter, you can grumble at your Fatherland as much as you please—but I love the Germans. Oh, how secretive they are and filled with divine forgetfulness! They cook their pea soup on blue gas flames and think nothing of it." Finally, the irrational takes command of Matern, as it had done at the radio interview, and he is provoked into throwing the pocket-knife into the water once more—not into the Vistula this time, but into the Landwehr Canal in Berlin, a place rich in bloody historical associations—and shouting, for the third time, "Itzich."

Matern has sinned, and Brauxel leads him into Hell (his potash mine). The first chronicler, Brauxel—the final resurrection of Amsel —turns out to be a figure of mysterious power in the German economy. His former potash mine has, typically for the postwar economy, turned from extractive to manufacturing indstury. Brauxel's mine produces scarecrows which represent parody of human activities and emotions, whereby the German situation is emphasized. The whole incident is broadly suggestive in several ways. In the first place, the journey into Hell is traditionally the descent into the unconscious. By eliciting from Matern the contemptuous yell against Jews, Brauxel has revealed to him his own hidden urges, so that it is appropriate that he should lead him down into a mine. The fact that the mine lies underneath Western Germany further suggests the haunting consciousness of the recent past.

Brauxel emphasizes this point by enrolling Hitler's dog as a Cerberus, a custodian of this underground company. Yet the scarecrows plainly have a significance that is not restricted to Germany, for, in primitive belief, the scarecrow, like the doll or the homuncule (both favorite motifs in Grass' works), is an image of the soul. Thus religion is a man-made thing and a manifestation of the nightmare world of the scarecrows as a mock theological dicussion shows: "If man was created in the image of God and the scarecrow in the image of man, is not then the scarecrow God's image?" (p. 670).

The human activities parodied by the scarecrows are, then, man's creations, while Amsel, the blackbird, represents man threatened by his own creations. These, especially the simpler models expressing hate and anger, find ready acceptance in the developing countries; and Amsel exports many scarecrows to the new African states.

The detailed parody of civilized man's activities begins with the manufacture of the scarecrows carried out in the first of the thirty-two sections of the mine. The preparation of their ragged clothes is dignified by means of a pretentious technical vocabulary into "Neustoffverunglimpfung" (textural detraction) carried out in

"Kaltzersetzungslaugen" (caustic solutions for cold decomposition). Mining terms, in which, as Leibniz remarked, the German language is particularly rich, are elaborately employed, even though Brauxel's mine ceased production in 1952. Here Grass has exploited his own experience in a potash mine near Hildesheim in 1946. This interpenetration of grotesqueness and reality is present in the lecturing style of the foreman, Wernicke. Despite the significance and gravity of the occasion, Matern reacts with the bewilderment and growing weariness of any visitor to an industrial plant.

Matern is led through all thirty-two chambers. The first six are devoted to the assembly of the scarecrows. In the following chambers the scarecrows acquire basic emotions, and in the last they apply these emotions to specific situations. Thus some chambers are devoted to sports and religion, others to family life; nor is Sex neglected. Philosophy is represented by Heidegger in his Alemannian nightcap, and Grass depicts him as being very much at home in this atmosphere of specialized and impenetrable jargon: "For the essence of scarecrowdom is the transcendentally arising threefold dispersion of scarecrows in the world projection" (p. 669).

The term "projection" is significant. In Heidegger's ontology the corresponding term "Entwurf" expresses the priority of possibility over the mode of reality: "Why does understanding—whatever may be the essential dimension of that which can be disclosed in it—always press forward into possibilities? It is because the understanding has in itself the existential structure which we call 'projection'." [6] The nightmare scarecrow world is one such "projection."

Ultimately the mine is an image representing the author himself, who draws his material from the depths of his mind to the surface, so that this novel can be considered a particularly choice scarecrow or, to revert to the imagery of the opening chapter, a bundle of rags floating past on the flooded Vistula. Both Brauxel and Matern, the author's creations, are drawn from the same repository of human characteristics where all possibilities are inherent and sharp distinctions, such as between victim and persecutor, are lost. Thus, after the ascent from the mine, the perspective wavers, so that it is uncertain whether Brauxel, Matern, or the author himself is speaking: "He leads me and him into cabins that contain Matern's and Brauxel's clothes. He and I get out of our miner's gear. The bathtubs are filled for me and him." The last sentence of the novel indicates the difficulties of communicating with others: "Eddi whistles something indistinct. I try to whistle something similar. But that is hard. We are both naked. Each of us bathes by himself" (p. 682).

CHAPTER 7

Grass' Political Writings

THE weakness of the latter part of *Hundejahre* lies in Grass' excessive propaganda zeal. The grotesqueness of Grass' world, which hitherto had served as a means of exploring reality, becomes a medium of political satire. Grass' satire fails because his world lacks a logic of its own. Once the reader of George Orwell's *Animal Farm* has accepted the fact that the animals control the farm, the parody of Stalinism follows naturally. In Grass' novels, on the other hand, the satirical point is imposed on a strange situation, such as that of miller Matern's mealworms being consulted as oracles by right-wing politicians.

Even without the now familiar newspaper reports of Grass' campaigns for the Socialist Party, his provocative speeches, and his appearances in the streets of Berlin selling newspapers, it is plain where his sympathies lie. Grass settled in Berlin in 1960 when he was awarded the Berlin Critics' Prize for *Die Blechtrommel*. In the election of 1961 he is said to have assisted Willy Brandt, the Socialist Mayor of West Berlin, in composing his speeches. In a pamphlet *Die Alternative*[1] (The Alternative), in which twenty-one authors expressed their belief in the need for a new government, Grass' contribution was an article addressed to nuns, advising them to vote for the Socialists: "Snap your fingers at the abbess." If he strikes a cheerful, even flippant, note here where seriousness might be expected, he disconcerts his audience at other times with partisan earnestness. When he was awarded the Georg Büchner Prize in 1965, just after the defeat of the Socialists, his address took the form of a startling attack on Erhard and German political indifference and complacency. He published the speech under the title *Rede über das Selbstverständliche* (On Matters That Are Taken For Granted).

Much of Gass' political activity is marked by this abhorrence of the cliché, of doing the correct and expected thing at the appropriate time. This is a characteristic of the amateur in politics: to the professional politician or journalist, concerned with the manipulation of the mass vote, the cliché is highly congenial. Gass' sincerity is patent. In the 1965 election campaign, on his own initiative and without financial support from the Socialist Party (in fact, in spite of the express disapproval of Wehnert, the Party organizer, as Grass assured his listeners), he made a tour of Western Germany in the hope of persuading "students, workers, nurses, soldiers and conservative old ladies wishing to do something progressive that it would be good for Germany if they voted for the Socialists in September." His campaign symbol, drawn and designed by him, was a cock crowing Es-Pe-De (SPD=Sozialistische Partei Deutschlands). Characteristically, Grass asked his audiences to imagine the cock as standing not on a church steeple (reserved for the rival Christian Democrats), but on a compost heap.

The cock reappears on the covers of three pamphlets containing the printed versions of Grass' speeches (and on a fourth pamphlet containing the Büchner Prize speech delivered later in the year in Darmstadt). Each pamphlet is introduced by a short essay entitled "Dich singe ich Demokratie"—a translation and adaptation of Walt Whitman's.

> For you these from me, O Democracy, to serve you, ma femme!
> For you, for you I am trilling these songs.

The introductory essay explains that Grass intends to use the profits from his campaign to acquire books for the West German Army. A note at the end of each pamphlet declares that profits from the sale of the pamphlets are to be used for the same purpose. Apparently, Grass does not share Max Frisch's skepticism concerning the influence of literature on human behavior.

The tone of the speeches is correspondingly idealist. Thus, "Was ist des Deutschen Vaterland?" (What is the German's Fatherland?), starting from a nineteenth-century patriotic poem by Ernst Moritz Arndt makes the delightful but impracticable suggestion that Germans should find a substitute for the regions lost after 1945 by founding towns in West Germany, to be called "New Danzig," "New Königsberg," "New Breslau," etc., where local dialects could be preserved, duly modified by the new surroundings. Grass carefully avoids professional solemnity. In the speech, "Loblied auf Willy," in which he defends Brandt against his detractors, he concludes with the exclamation, "Pack den Willy in den Tank!"—an echo of the then current Esso slogan, "Pack a tiger in your tank." The third pamphlet, "Es steht zur Wahl" (We Have the Choice), begins by dismissing the political prospects of Franz-Josef Strauss, who was notorious for his undemocratic methods in the "*Spiegel* affair," but this reveals Grass' political naïveté: Strauss became Finance Minister in the 1966 Coalition Government. Grass also contributed a poem to a paperback *Plädoyer für eine neue Regierung* (Pleadings for a New Government).[2] Hochhuth's attack on Erhard in this booklet provoked the latter into rebuking Hochhuth as a "little terrier." Grass responded by calling Erhard a "Banause."

Grass' three campaign speeches, as well as his Darmstadt address, make extensive reference to the division of Germany and to the East German revolt of June 17, 1953—uncomfortable subjects which both politicians and public have agreed to pass over in silence. Grass refused to do this. In the Darmstadt address he complains that the question of buying a second car occupies the public far more than the question of reunification. Concerning the revolt, Grass declares that Ulbricht, the East German leader, and Adenauer, the late West German Chancellor, "two mutually dependent deadly enemies," have both misrepresented the event for their own purposes. In all three speeches, Grass condemns as hypocritical the act of the West German government in declaring June 17 a public holiday when, at the time, they had not only done nothing to guide, advise, or support the movement, but had done their best to overlook it as something embarrassing. It is evident that the uprising occupied Grass' thoughts during the 1965 election campaign.

This interest had been more opportunely displayed in a speech delivered in the Berlin Akademie der Kunst during the 1964 "Shakespeare Year" and published in *Akzente* under the title "Vor- und Nachgeschichte der Tragödie des Coriolanus von Livius und Plutarch über Shakespeare bis zu Brecht und mir" (Previous and Subsequent History of the Tragedy of Coriolanus from Livy and Plutarch by Way of Shakespeare to Brecht and Me).[3] The essential passage of this rambling discourse comes at the end where Grass mentions being struck by the fact that Brecht was working on his adaptation of Shakespeare's *Coriolanus* during the years 1952 and 1953, with the ironic result that while Brecht was racking his brains attempting, with the aid of the "dialectics of the theater," to lend power and conviction to Shakespeare's contemptible plebs, the real plebs, without his help, were engaged in a revolt against the work norms imposed by tyrannical rulers. (As a matter of historical fact, on the day of the uprising—June 17, 1953—Brecht was engaged in rehearsing an entirely different play.) "This would be a good starting point for a play that could be called *The Plebeians Rehearse the Uprising*," Grass observes.

It is apparent that he has gone a long way toward planning the drama, for he goes on to describe how "in my play" the workers appear at the rehearsal and ask the Director (Chef) to compose for them a call to a general strike. Although the Director does not refuse point blank, he does ask them for a demonstration of how the strike had begun among the building workers on the Stalinallee. He hopes, Grass explains, to utilize the workers' account of what had happened for stage purposes. The workers want to win him over to their cause, but Brecht uses the workers to help him with his theatrical problems. Thus, when the workers talk of the East German leaders Ulbricht and Grotewohl, the Director counters with the Roman tribunes Sicinius and Brutus; when the workers (apparently not reduced to the helpless stupidity they display in Grass' play) talk of Marx, the Director tells of Livy. Irony resides in the fact that while the Director is thoroughly confident of the victory of his stage plebs, the real workers are full of hesitation. Finally, when the uprising is crushed by Russian tanks, the Director considers the experiment of introducing tanks onto the stage. Conscious, perhaps, that the dénouement sounds feeble, Grass lapses at the end of his essay into curt, incomplete phrases that recall his parody of the *Oberstudienrat* in *Katz und Maus*: "Wheat prices and high norms. Construction workers' and plebs' revolt. . . . History and its adaptation. Literary property and its owners. The national holiday and the Shakespeare Year: this play must be written."

The play was written and duly performed in Berlin on January 15, 1966. The promising original idea has been retained. The Director is rehearsing his version of *Coriolanus* when the actors, including the actress who is playing Volumnia, modeled after Brecht's wife Helene Weigel, arrive late with reports of demonstrations at the construction sites of the Stalinallee. Suddenly, in the midst of the colorful Shakespearian costumes, appear the rebellious laborers in their working clothes. They ask the Director to write a manifesto in support of their cause: he is world famous, they tell him, and his word carries weight with the regime. However, the Director has only contempt for the "ungeprobte Zappelei" (unrehearsed floundering).[4] What interests him, he explains to Volumnia, is the behavior of the rebels because he may be able to utilize this knowledge in staging the revolt scenes in his play. While Volumnia pleads with him not to play the remote Chinese mandarin, the wise Chinese of certain of Brecht's poems and anecdotes, the Director persuades the reluctant workers to give him a demonstration of their rebellion on the stage. At this point, Kosanke appears. He is the official Party poet (his real-life equivalent is a certain Kuba), and he comes with a request from the Government that the Director address the rebels and urge them to disperse. The Director refuses, and Kosanke is driven from the theater amidst the jeers of both workers and actors.

A new delegation arrives—delegates sent from Eastern Germany by the leaders of the revolt. They, too, want the Director's manifesto and they tell him of the spread of the strike beyond East Berlin. Some of them decide that the Director's hesitation marks him as a traitor to the cause, and they peremptorily prepare to hang him together with Erwin, his literary editor (*Dramaturg*). At that point, instead of congratulating the rebels for their stern professionalism, the Director condemns them for producing bad drama. Erwin, however, shows that drama has its uses. He rescues himself and his Director by reciting a variation of the famous parable of "the belly and the members," spoken by Menenius in Shakespeare's *Coriolanus*. The rebellion, then, sends new messengers in the form of a young girl, a hairdresser, who drags in a wounded man—the man who had pulled down the Communist flag from the Brandenburg Gate in the center of Berlin. Real life shows that it can compete with the theater. Russian tanks are heard, together with the voice of Kosanke exhorting the crowd, but the girl's enthusiasm almost succeeds in converting the Director. He is nearly prepared to go out onto the streets with her when Volumnia arrives and announces the failure of the rebellion. While the workers and actors leave, the Director is left alone with his sense of guilt:

> Es atmete der heilge Geist
> Ich hielt's für Zugluft,
> rief: wer stört. (p. 92)

("The breath of the Holy Ghost—I took it for a draft and called out: stop bothering me.")

Erwin returns in the fourth and final act to confirm the failure of the revolt. Two stage assistants, Podulla and Litthenner, start to imitate Soviet tanks with the help of chairs on stage (it is no longer the Director himself but his students who now consider recent events from the point of view of stagecraft). Actors enter with reports about the rebellion and tell how unarmed men attacked tanks. Kosanke comes to gloat, but is prepared to be content with a message of congratulation to the Government; Volumnia had interceded with him in behalf of the Director. However, Kosanke is sent away empty-handed, pursued by the laughter of the theater folk. They had trapped him in a dialectical quibble, although, as Erwin points out, this jeopardizes the future of the theater.

In the meantime, the Director has been writing an address to the Government. Volumnia reads it and assures him that the Communist authorities will publish only the harmless first paragraph. This, again, is a reflection of what really happened to Brecht who had sent a long, closely argued letter to Ulbricht. Only the last sentence, "I feel the need to express to you at this moment my attachment to the Socialist Unity Party," was published.

Volumnia sums up the influence that the Director will leave on posterity: "Really he was against it. Rather, for it, really. He *said* this but his heart was . . ." (p. 104). The Director will soon retire to the country to write poetry. He remains alone with the tape-recorder on which he has recorded many of the preceding scenes, but none of them will be used for the stage. His final words are an echo from Brecht's posthumously published poem, "Böser Morgen": "Unwissende! Ihr Unwissende! Schuldbewusst klage ich euch an" ("You ignorant people! Conscious of my own guilt, I denounce you").

The basic flaw in the play is immediately apparent from the summary. Its plot, its whole conception preclude development of any real action, Brecht did not intervene in the uprising, the Director must remain similarly inactive. In each of the four acts, the plot threatens to grind to a halt despite attempts to inject movement and action. A bricklayer suddenly starts to destroy a cardboard portrait of Stalin; a fresh delegation arrives and prepares to hang the Director and his assistant (a strangely listless scene); a wounded man is dragged on stage with a flag from the Brandenburg Gate.

The real theme of the play is the failure of communication between the Director and the people. The Director regards the workers with the contempt of a Marxist for whom revolution is an art to be practiced by an elite. As a man of the theater, he points out to Kosanke, the workers have failed to rehearse:

Hör zu: im Bett die lust'ge Liebe,
die Taufe später, mühevoll der Tod,
den Krieg, den Frieden muss man proben,
die Hasenjagd, das Fussballspiel,
sogar das Chaos muss man proben. (p. 59)

("Listen. Lusty love in bed, the christening later, death painfully, war, peace must be rehearsed. Hunting the hare, playing football, even chaos must be rehearsed.")

While he keeps the workers waiting for the manifesto that is never forthcoming, he never seems to tire of taunting them as revolutionaries who are frightened to walk on the grass. The incredible climax is reached when the Director employs the workers for a stage sketch he has devised, containing, among others, this couplet:

Drum werden die Revolutionäre gebeten
den städtischen Rasen nicht zu betreten. (p. 53)

("Revolutionaries are asked to refrain from walking on the grass.")

Only at this point does one of the workers throw down the banner he has been carrying and shout, "We are not a lot of tailor's dummies!" But this is just what the workers are. Even now, when they refuse to go on acting, the Director records their insults on tape and points out how they could swear more effectively. Even when they prepare to hang him, the Director cannot take the workers seriously. The result is that neither can the audience take the scene seriously.

Hans Mayer sees in the Director a demonstration of the failure to accept responsibility.[5] It is probably simpler to consider the relationship between the Director and the workers as typical of the gap between the intellectuals and the common people, between fully-blown academic theory and ill-considered practice. One of the workers sums up the Director's unwillingness to help their cause when he compares the Director to the University staff and students whom the workers had failed to stir to political action earlier in the day: "He is letting the shutters down, just as they did in the University." This lack of contact, a characteristic German failing in the political sphere, lends point to the subtitle of the play, "A German Tragedy." (The term "tragedy," as Mayer points out, is justified because Grass observes the Aristotelian unities of time and place.)

The failure is all the more ironical in view of the fact that it is the precise aim of Brecht's "dialectical theater" to reveal the contradictions in the existing social order and thus to encourage the public to remedy these defects. "What we must achieve," Brecht once said at a writers' conference, "is the creation of militancy in the audience, the militancy of the new against the old." [6] The Director's stage in this play, with its incongruous mixture of actors in Roman costumes and real proletarians—the two parties at one point actually come to blows—suggests the failure of this aim.

The effectiveness of this piece of irony depends on some knowledge of Brecht's theories, for without the parallel to Brecht, the central figure of the play is ghostly indeed. Yet this parallel can never be developed in dramatic terms because Grass' Director has no dialogue partner. The workers are as naïve as children, the Party poet Kosanke a figure of fun, and Volumnia merely provides a cue for ironic utterances. In the course of Grass' play, the Director adopts a succession of roles, none of them especially Brechtian. At times he is the hardened revolutionary, pointing out to the workers their elementary mistakes: "Have you occupied the radio station? Called a general strike?" At other times he is Hamlet. The written statements he produces after Wiebe and Damaschke have arrived from headquarters ("Fine names, like Rosencrantz and Guildenstern") are replete with Hamlet's irony. The workers bring out the Coriolanus in him ("Kneaders of dough who want to make a saber-rattling hero out of me"), although at times the irony is borrowed from Brecht himself. Thus the Director's:

> Und wenn Dir dieses Volk nicht passt
> dann wähl dir eins, das besser passt. (p. 73)

addressed to Ulbricht, is an echo of Brecht's poem, "Die Lösung" (The Solution): "Would it not be simpler if the Government dissolved the people and elected another?" [7]

To Coriolanus and Hamlet is added the man of impulse, moved to join the revolt by the enthusiasm of a young hairdresser's assistant who reports how the Director's plays have moved her (she quotes from Brecht's *Mother Courage*): "There—there I sat when Kattrin sat on the roof up here, dumb, and beat the drum, as I now cry: Tanks are coming" (p. 89). When Volumnia persuades him that it is too late to join the revolution, the Director's behavior becomes strangely inconsistent. While he refuses to sign Kosanke's declaration of loyalty, yet he writes a letter to the authorities, knowing that it will be misused for propaganda purposes (as, in fact, a letter from Brecht is assumed to have been misused).[8] The play concludes with the Director's insoluble conflict implicit in Brecht's posthumously published "Böser Morgen": "Last night I saw fingers pointing at me as at a leper. They were work-gnarled and broken. 'You don't know,' I cried, conscious of my own guilt." [9] In this sense, then, the Director is—somewhat like Frisch's Stiller—torn between many possible roles. At one point he confirms this interpretation by calling out, somewhat theatrically, "What's the creature called? What's it called? Changes its color at will? Chameleon! That's it—chameleon! No! How often do you think I can keep chopping and changing" (p. 99). Here, then, is a further promising theme that is not developed.

Yet even if the play as a whole lacks theatrical conviction (and critics were fairly unanimous on this point), certain passages are successful in evoking current history on the stage. The rough blank-verse account of the origins of the rebellion, for example, matches the everyday language:

> Nein, erst beim Frühstück ging's von Mund zu Mund
> Es kamen die vom Block C-Süd
> wir vom Block vierzig wussten schon
> weil wir vor Tagen auf dem Müggelsee
> auf einem Dampfer, auf Betriebsausflug
> uns abgesprochen haben . . . (p. 26)

("No, it was at breakfast that word first went around. They came from Block C South; we in Block forty knew all about it because we'd arranged it days before during an outing on the Müggelsee . . .")

Toward the end of the play, the actors describe the Russian tanks on the streets of Berlin: "And one man—I saw it myself—rolled up his briefcase and shoved it up the exhaust pipe." Another striking aspect of the rebellion was (and is) the indifference of most West Germans. This, too, is discussed in blank verse:

> That's it. They'll not bestir themselves one bit.
> Although they'll put (it doesn't cost them much)
> Some candles in the window once a year. (p. 69)

The Director's epitaph on the uprising sums up the whole grossly misrepresented event:

Bricklayers, railway workers, welders, and cable layers fought alone. Housewives did not want to be mere onlookers. Even policemen took off their belts and joined in. They are certain to be punished summarily. Our prisons will not be big enough in East Germany. But on the other side, too, there will be official lying. The face of hypocrisy will carefully practice an expression of mourning and deep concern. My prophetic eye sees national rags at halfmast. (p. 104)

The Director foresees the day when June 17 will be a national holiday in West Germany, celebrated by an increased number of traffic accidents.

The views that Grass expresses in this play are those of a liberal-minded intellectual. He dislikes both German governments, East and West, and deplores the materialism of the prosperous West German society. He both admires and distrusts Brecht. However, enlightened opinions and uncomfortable truths strikingly stated do not, in themselves, make a good play.

CHAPTER 8

Summary

GRASS' reputation rests chiefly on his fiction. His poetry, especially his early poetry, is often tentative in character, as if he were experimenting with images that suggest the absurdity or precariousness of the human condition. The absurd plays, attempts to clarify and develop such images, are aptly characterized by Martin Esslin as "metaphors come to life on the stage." [1] *Hochwasser,* for example, probably Grass' most successful play, clarifies the cryptic imagery of the poem by the same name. *Beritten hin und zurück* and *Noch zehn Minuten bis Buffalo* present an absurd world in terms of infantile farce. *Onkel, Onkel* retains the farce, but emphasizes the irrational powers that dominate human affairs. *Die bösen Köche* uses images associated with kitchens and cooks to represent the tragicomic hopelessness of the quest for spiritual nourishment.

This, Grass' most ambitious absurd play, is heavily symbolical and reduces the images to symbols that illustrate the central statement. Only in his fiction, however, do Grass' images reveal their full significance when placed in the context of Danzig during the Nazi era. The Danzig setting provides the factual background which the novel form demands, the *terra incognita* which the author explores, as Joyce explores Dublin, or Faulkner the South.

Grass spent his childhood in Danzig. Yet, even though this childhood world has been irrevocably swept away, his matter-of-fact descriptions dispense with any tender appeal to the universal experience of mankind. This refusal to abandon the concrete and particular object or event for abstract ideas and sentiments is characteristic of Grass' approach. He does not pause in his narrative to point to the infantile, bestial, or lower-middle-class elements of the Nazi movement or to persuade the reader that human reason has little part in human history. These considerations are woven into the narrative itself, into its structure, its plot, and into apparently insignificant details of the setting. As far as Grass' narrators are concerned, it is the story itself—long and drawn out (except in *Katz und Maus*), involved and full of accurately observed detail—which is of overriding importance.

Actually, however, the manner in which the stories are told is never as unsophisticated as the narrators' deportment suggests. Grass delights, for instance, in parody, which places his statements in a wider context, and in comments on the part of the narrator, somewhat in the manner of Sterne or Jean Paul, which destroy the illusion that the novels are "life" and not "art." These devices, however, are never so dominant that the thread of the narrative is lost. Again, Grass frequently jumps backwards or forwards in time, or varies the tempo of his narrative, now proceeding at a rapid pace, now lingering on some event or motif. Thus, in the opening passage of *Hundejahre*, the narrator lingers over a description of the Vistula, and in this way draws attention to the formless flow of time which is the raw material that the novelist must shape. Yet not even in this slowly moving passage is the narrative impulse lost. The narrator never loses sight of the individual features of the main actors or of the Vistula landscape.[2]

Behind the fictitious narrator, who is totally absorbed in his narrative, is the real narrator, the novelist himself, whose presence is hinted at in the opening passages of *Die Blechtrommel* and *Hundejahre*, for example. The novelist's comments and reflections, his fears, disgust, and sympathy are all absorbed into the people and objects of the novels, which thus take on a grotesque character. Although the people and the objects are real enough as participants in the fictitious narrator's story, at the same time they express Grass' view of the world in which they live; and it is this double nature that gives Grass' novels their characteristic pervasive irony. Oskar, Maria, Tulla, and Harras gravely go about their trivial everyday business, while neither they nor the fictitious narrators seem aware that they are exponents of the larger world. In *Katz und Maus*, in which the grotesque element is kept within the limits of the possible, the irony arising from the unawareness of the hero's relationship to his times is especially important.

When *Die Blechtrommel* and *Hundejahre* deal with Western Germany, Grass' indignation and sense of political engagement come to the fore. The author who created out of the prewar era the vision of an absurd world without values now seems disconcertingly inclined to allow his voice to be heard in judgment and condemnation of West German personalities and institutions. His concern with political issues finds expression in his private campaign for the Socialist Party and in the political pamphlets he wrote. The question of the Berlin uprising of 1953, raised in these pamphlets, is taken up again in the play *Die Plebejer proben den Aufstand.* Grass' latest volume of verse, *Ausgefragt,* contains political poems and protest (much of it directed against the war in Vietnam) together with verses that express an awareness of the futility of protest. For example, the poem "Irgendwas machen" (Do Something About It) contains these lines: "I speak of the wooden sword and the missing tooth, of the protest poem."

At his best, Grass avoids direct protest and follows the precepts laid down by Max Frisch in his *Diary:*

What is important, the inexpressible, the blank between the words, and these words always speak of incidentals that we do not really mean. The real point, what we really want to say, can best be approached indirectly, by circumlocution; which means that one writes around the subject. One makes statements that never contain what one really experiences, which remains inexpressible. These statements can only outline it, as nearly and accurately as possible, and the real point, the inexpressible, appears at best suspended between the statements.[3]

Notes and References

Page references to quotations from Grass' novels appear parenthetically in the text after each quotation. Translations are by the author of this monograph. The texts used are: *Die Blechtrommel* (Darmstadt, Berlin and Neuwied: Luchterhand, 1959); *Katz und Maus* (Neuwied and Berlin: Luchterhand, 1961); *Hundejahre* (Neuwied and Berlin: Luchterhand, 1963).

Introduction

1. Thomas Mann, *Gesammelte Werke*, vol. VI (Frankfurt, 1960), pp. 668–676.
2. Walter Muschg, *Die Zerstörung der deutschen Literatur* (Bern, 1958).
3. Hans Schwab-Felisch, "Literatur der Obergefreiten," *Der Monat*, IV (1952), 664; Helmut Günther, "Die deutsche Kriegsliteratur 1945–1952," *Welt und Wort*, VIII (1953), p. 179.
4. Heinrich Böll, "Bekenntnis zur Trümmerliteratur" in *Hierzulande: Aufsätze zur Zeit* (Munich, 1963), pp. 128–134.
5. Walter Jens, *Deutsche Literatur der Gegenwart* (Munich, 1961), p. 78.
6. *Ibid.*, p. 150.
7. *Ibid.*, p. 81.

Chapter 1

1. Jens, p. 151.
2. Friedrich Schlegel, *Kritische Schriften* (Munich, 1956), p. 139.
3. Klaus Wagenbach, "Günter Grass" in *Schriftsteller der Gegenwart*, ed. Klaus Nonnemann (Olten and Freiburg, 1963), p. 124.
4. Walter H. Sokel, *The Writer in Extremis* (Stanford, 1959), pp. 46 f.

5. (H.-M.) Enzensberger, "Günter Grass' *Hundejahre*," *Der Spiegel*, September 4, 1963, p. 71.
6. H.-M. Enzensberger, *Frankfurter Hefte*, XI (1959), 833.
7. Wolfgang Kayser, *Das sprachliche Kunstwerk* (Bern, 1948), p. 365.
8. Martin Esslin, *The Theatre of the Absurd* (New York, 1961), p. 293.
9. Wagenbach, pp. 125 f. Further discussed by Erika Metzer-Hirt in *Monatshefte*, LVII (1965), 283–290.
10. *Akzente*, IV (1957), 229.

Chapter 2

1. Günter Grass, *Die Vorzüge der Windhühner* (Berlin and Neuwied, 1956).
2. For biographical details, see the article in *Der Spiegel*, September 4, 1963, pp. 64–78.
3. *Akzente*, II (1955), 259 f.
4. For a discussion of Grass' illustrations, see Adolph Wegener in *Philobiblon*, X (June, 1966), 110–117.
5. Günter Grass, *Die Ballerina* (Berlin, 1963).
6. Günter Grass, *Gleisdreieck* (Darmstadt, Berlin and Neuwied, 1961).
7. Marie Luise Kaschnitz, *Neue Gedichte* (Hamburg, 1957), p. 12.
8. Günter Grass, *Ausgefragt* (Neuwied and Berlin, 1967).
9. Gottfried Benn, *Probleme der Lyrik* (Wiesbaden, 1951), p. 16.

Chapter 3

1. Quoted by Kurt Lothar Tank, *Günter Grass* (Berlin, 1965), p. 37.
2. *Akzente*, V (1958), 399–409.

3. *Akzente,* VII (1960), 498–539, and Günter Grass, *Hochwasser,* edition suhrkamp (Frankfurt, 1963).

4. Bertolt Brecht, "Bei Durchsicht meiner ersten Stücke," introductory essay to *Stücke,* I (Berlin, 1954).

5. *Hochwasser,* p. 60.

6. *Ibid.,* p. 77.

7. Wilhelm Emrich, "Zur Ästhetik der modernen Dichtung," *Akzente,* IV (1954), p. 312.

8. The first act of the first version was published in *Text + Kritik,* No. 1 (no date), pp. 17–24.

9. Günter Grass, *Onkel, Onkel* (Berlin, 1965), p. 10.

10. *Ibid.,* p. 28.

11. *Ibid.,* p. 45.

12. *Ibid.,* p. 72.

13. Marianne Kesting, *Panorama des zeitgenössischen Theaters* (Munich, 1962), p. 254.

14. *Onkel, Onkel,* p. 34.

15. Wolfgang Hildesheimer, "Erlanger Rede," *Akzente,* VIII (1960), 543.

16. *Modernes deutsches Theater* 1, ed. Paul Pörtner (Neuwied and Berlin, 1961), p. 66.

17. See "Grass-Premiere: In der Küche," *Der Spiegel,* March 1, 1961, p. 77.

18. Esslin, p. 196.

19. *Modernes deutsches Theater,* p. 72.

20. For further discussion, see Peter Spycher, "*Die bösen Köche* von Günter Grass—ein absurdes Drama?" *Germanisch-Romanische Monatsschrift,* XVI (1966), 161 ff.

21. Kesting, p. 255.

22. Tank, p. 40.

Chapter 4

1. Allan Bullock, *Hitler: A Study in Tyranny* (London, 1962), p. 117.

2. Bertolt Brecht, *Gedichte,* V (Frankfurt, 1964), 128.

3. For a contrary opinion, see A.

Leslie Willson in *Monatshefte,* LVIII (1966), 133.

4. See the interview with Grass in the *Saturday Review,* May 29, 1965, p. 26.

5. Stefan Zweig, *Die Welt von Gestern* (Frankfurt, 1955), p. 13.

6. Gottfried Benn, "Ikarus," *Die gesammelten Schriften* (Berlin, 1922), p. 38.

7. C. G. Jung, *Psychologische Abhandlungen,* IV (Zurich, 1948), 434.

8. Ernst Toller, *Prosa Briefe Dramen Gedichte* (Reinbeck, 1961), p. 405.

9. Erich Maria Remarque, *Der schwarze Obelisk* (Cologne and Berlin, 1956), p. 234.

10. Peter Weiss, *Die Verfolgung und Ermordung Jean Paul Marats . . .* (Frankfurt, 1966), p. 46.

Chapter 5

1. Quoted by Ernest J. Simmons in *Dostoievsky* (New York, 1962), p. 197.

2. H.-M. Enzensberger, *Frankfurter Hefte,* XII (1961), 197.

3. Herbert Ahl, *Literarische Porträts* (Munich and Vienna, 1962), p. 33.

4. Wilhelm Duwe, *Deutsche Dichtung des 20. Jahrhunderts* (Zurich, 1962), p. 158.

5. For further details about the film see *Der Spiegel,* December 22, 1966, p. 22.

Chapter 6

1. Bobrowski devotes a poem to Thomas in *Sarmatische Zeit* (Stuttgart, 1961), p. 48.

2. Johannes Bobrowski, *Levins Mühle* (Frankfurt, 1964).

3. Alfred Döblin, *Berlin Alexanderplatz* (Olten and Freiburg, 1961), pp. 31 f.

4. *Das Atelier,* ed. Klaus Wagenbach (Frankfurt, 1962), pp. 41–54.

5. Golo Mann, *Deutsche Geschichte 1919–1945* (Frankfurt, 1961), p. 195.

Notes and References

6. Martin Heidegger, *Being and Time*, trans. John Macquarrie and Edward Robinson (London, 1962), p. 144.

Chapter 7

1. *Die Alternative*, ed. Martin Walser (Reinbeck, 1961).
2. Ed. Hans Werner Richter (Reinbeck, 1965).
3. *Akzente*, XI (1964), 194–221.
4. Günter Grass, *Die Plebejer proben den Aufstand* (Neuwied and Berlin, 1966), p. 20. The numbers in parentheses refer to the pages of this edition. Translations are by the author of this monograph.
5. Hans Mayer in *Theater Heute* (March, 1966), p. 23.
6. Speech given at the Fourth East German Writers' Conference held in January, 1956, and published in *Beiträge zur Gegenwarts-literatur*, I (Berlin, 1956).
7. Quoted by W. Paul, *Neue Deutsche Hefte* (November, 1958), p. 711.
8. Martin Esslin, *Brecht* (New York, 1961), p. 182.
9. Dated 1953 and published in *Sinn und Form* (Zweites Sonderheft Bertolt Brecht, 1957), p. 341.

Chapter 8

1. Martin Esslin in his introduction to *Four Plays by Günter Grass*, trans. Ralph Mannheim (London and New York, 1967).
2. Walter Höllerer, "Die Bedeutung des Augenblicks im modernen Romananfang," in *Romananfänge* (Berlin, 1965), pp. 370 f.
3. Max Frisch, *Tagebuch 1946–1949* (Frankfurt, 1950), p. 411.

Selected Bibliography

I PRIMARY SOURCES

Die Vorzüge der Windhühner (Berlin and Neuwied: Luchterhand, 1956).

Die Blechtrommel (Darmstadt, Berlin and Neuwied: Luchterhand, 1959). First paperback edition: Fischer, 1962.

Gleisdreieck (Darmstadt, Berlin and Neuwied: Luchterhand, 1960).

Die bösen Köche in *Modernes deutsches Theater I*, ed. Paul Pörtner (Neuwied and Berlin: Luchterhand, 1961).

Katz und Maus (Neuwied and Berlin: Luchterhand, 1961). First paperback edition: Rowohlt, 1963.

Hundejahre (Neuwied and Berlin: Luchterhand, 1963).

Hochwasser (Frankfurt: Suhrkamp, 1963).

Die Ballerina (Berlin: Luchterhand, 1963).

Onkel, Onkel (Berlin: Klaus Wagenbach, 1965).

Was ist des Deutschen Vaterland, Es steht zur Wahl, Loblied auf Willy and *Rede über das Selbstverständliche* (Neuwied and Berlin: Luchterhand, 1965).

Die Plebejer proben den Aufstand (Neuwied and Berlin: Luchterhand, 1966).

Ausgefragt (Neuwied and Berlin: Luchterhand, 1967).

Published in *Akzente*, a literary periodical edited by Walter Höllerer and Hans Bender. Most of the poems printed here reappear in the poetry volumes.

II (1955). Poems: "Lilien aus Schlaf" (pp. 259–260) and "Kürzestgeschichten aus Berlin" (p. 517). Prose passage: "Meine grüne Wiese" (pp. 528–534).

III (1956). Poem (pp. 432–435) and "Die Ballerina/Dichtung und Mimus" (pp. 531–539).

IV (1957). "Der Inhalt als Widerstand/Bausteine zur Poetik" (pp. 229–235).

V (1958). "Noch zehn Minuten bis Buffalo" (pp. 5–17). Poems (pp. 59–61 and pp. 387–388). "Beritten hin und zurück" (pp. 399–409).

VI (1959). Extracts from *Die Blechtrommel* (pp. 2–35). Poems (pp. 483–487).

VII (1960). Poems (pp. 48–49, pp. 262–265 and p. 435). First version of "Hochwasser" (pp. 498–539).

VIII (1961). Poems (pp. 7–8). Critical essay "Das Gelegenheitsgedicht" (pp. 8–11) and extract from *Hundejahre* ("Kartoffelschalen") (pp. 196–206).

X (1963). Extract from *Hundejahre* (pp. 22–33).

XI (1964). "Vor- und Nachgeschichte der Tragödie des Coriolanus von Livius und Plutarch über Shakespeare bis zu Brecht und mir" (pp. 194–221).

XII (1965). Poems (pp. 122–123 and p. 289).

XIII (1966). Poems (pp. 200–207, 481–489 and 578–579) and critical essay "Vom mangelnden Selbstvertrauen der schreibenden Hofnarren" (pp. 194–199).

Miscellaneous

"Die Linkshänder," *Neue Deutsche Hefte*, V (1958/59), 38–42, reprinted in *Deutschland erzählt*, ed. Benno von Wiese (Frankfurt, 1962).

"Meine grüne Wiese," *Deutsche Prosa, Erzählungen seit 1945*, ed. Horst Bingel (Stuttgart, 1963).

Hochwasser and *Noch zehn Minuten bis Buffalo* ed. Leslie Wllson (New York: Appleton-Century-Crofts, 1967). An annotated edition for American students.

English translations of Grass' works by Ralph Mannheim (published simultaneously in London and New York: Harcourt, Brace and World).

The Tin Drum, 1962.

Cat and Mouse, 1963.

Dog Years, 1965.

The Plebeians Rehearse the Uprising, 1966. With an introductory address by Grass and a documentary report on June 17, 1953, by Ula Gerhardt.

Four Plays (Flood; Mister, Mister; Only Ten Minutes to Buffalo; The Wicked Cooks), 1967. With an introduction by Martin Esslin.

In German with English translations by Michael Hamburger and Christopher Middleton:

Selected Poems, 1966.

Über das Selbstverständliche (Neuwied and Berlin: Luchterhand, 1968).

Über meinen Lehrer Döblin und andere Vorträge (Berlin: Literarisches Colloquium, 1968).

II SECONDARY SOURCES

HERBERT AHL, *Literarische Porträts* (Munich and Vienna, 1961), pp. 28–25.

JAMES C. BRUCE, "The Equivocating Narrator in Günter Grass' *Katz und Maus*," *Monatshefte*, LVIII (1966), 139–149.

HANS MAGNUS ENZENSBERGER, *Einzelheiten* (Frankfurt, 1962), pp. 221–

233 (on *Die Blechtrommel*); *Frankfurter Hefte*, XII (1961), 860 (on *Katz und Maus*).

MARTIN ESSLIN, *The Theatre of the Absurd* (New York, 1961), pp. 195 ff. On Grass' absurd drama.

ERHARD M. FRIEDRICHSMEYER, "Aspects of Myth, Parody and Obscenity in Günter Grass' *Die Blechtrommel* and *Katz und Maus*," *Germanic Review*, XL (1965), 240–247.

MANFRED GÜNSEL, in *Blätter und Bilder*, XII (1961), p. 79. A parody of Grass.

HELMUT HEISSENBÜTTEL, *Über Literatur* (Olten and Freiburg, 1966). On modern literature with passing mention of Grass.

ERIKA METZGER-HIRT, "Günter Grass 'Askese': Eine Interpretation," *Monatshefte*, LVIII (1965), 238–290.

WALTER HÖLLERER, "Die Bedeutung des Augenblicks im modernen Romananfäng," in *Romananfänge—Versuch einer Poetik des Romans* (Berlin, 1965). Contains discussion of the opening of *Hundejahre*.

K. A. HORST, in *Merkur*, XIII (1959) 1191–1195; XV (1961), 1197 f. and XVII (1963), 1003–1008. Reviews of Grass' novels.

WALTER JENS, *Deutsche Literatur der Gegenwart* (Munich, 1961). On modern German literature with mention of Grass.

MARIANNE KESTING, *Panorama des zeitgenössischen Theaters* (Munich, 1962), pp. 253 ff. Critical of Grass' absurd plays.

PAUL KONRAD KURZ, *Über moderne Literatur* (Frankfurt, 1967), pp. 158–176. On *Hundejahre*, reprinted from *Stimmen der Zeit*, II (1963/64).

HANS MAYER, *Theater heute* (March, 1966), pp. 23–26. Comparison of Grass' *Plebejer* with Dürrenmatt's *Meteor*.

KARL MIGNER, *Welt und Wort*, XV (1960), 205 f. Review of *Die Blechtrommel*, stressing religious aspects.

Selected Bibliography

ILPO TAPANI PIIRAINEN, *Textbezogene Untersuchungen über "Katz und Maus" und "Hundejahre" von Günter Grass* (Münster/Westfalen, 1966). Criticism of Grass on aesthetic grounds.

PAUL PÖRTNER, "Nachwort" to the volume *Modernes deutsches Theater* (Neuwied and Berlin, 1961). Deals with Grass' *Die bösen Köche*.

MARCEL REICH-RANICKI, *Deutsche Literatur in West und Ost* (Munich, 1963). Passing mention of Grass in a general, popular discussion of modern German literature. See also the reviews in *Die Zeit* of January 25, 1966 and May 23. 1967.

KARL RIHA, *Moritat. Song. Bänkelsang* (Göttingen, 1965), pp. 159 ff. On Grass' poem "Annabel Lee."

KARL H. RUHLEDER, "A Pattern of Messianic Thought in Günter Grass' *Katz und Maus*," *German Quarterly* XXXIX (1966), 599–612.

PETER SPYCHER, "*Die bösen Köche* von Günter Grass—ein absurdes Drama?" *Germanisch-Romanische Monatsschrift*, XVI (1966), 161–173.

KURT LOTHAR TANK, *Günter Grass* (Berlin: Colloquium Verlag, 1965), the most complete study of Grass' works published to date.

KLAUS WAGENBACH in *Schriftsteller der Gegenwart: 53 Porträts*, ed. Klaus Nonnemann (Olten and Freiburg, 1963), pp. 118–126. An excellent brief analysis.

ADOLPH WEGENER, "Lyrik und Graphik von Günter Grass," *Philobiblon*, X (1966), 110–117.

ERNST WENDT, "Sein grosses Ja . . . ," *Theater heute* (April, 1967), pp. 6–11. On Grass' *Plebejer*.

ROLAND H. WIEGENSTEIN, in *Frankfurter Hefte*, XII (1963), 870 ff. Review of *Hundejahre*.

A. LESLIE WILLSON, "The Grotesque Everyman in Günter Grass's *Die Blechtrommel*," *Monatshefte*, LVIII (1960), 131–138.

See also the first issue of the periodical *Text + Kritik* (no date) devoted to Günter Grass.

For biographical details, see *Der Spiegel*, September 4, 1963, pp. 64–78.

Index